Practice Aloha

Practice Aloha
Secrets to Living Life Hawaiian Style

Stories, Recipes and Lyrics
from Hawai'i's Favorite Folks

Compiled & Edited by
Mark Ellman & Barbara Santos
with Tehani Kahaialii-Taulava

Photos edited and contributed by
Tony Novak-Clifford

Mutual Publishing

Tony Novak-Clifford edited the photos for this book.

Cover photo: Sunrise at Manana (Rabbit Island) by Patrick Ching
Live Aloha/Pink Plumeria (page 7) by Randy Jay Braun
Trini, Linda, Elisa, and Barbara photo (page 97) by Will Southard
Shirley Fong-Torres photo (page 103) by Frank Jang
Keola Beamer photo (page 109) by Guy Sibilla
Jay Larrin photo (page 130) by Edwin B. Kayton

ISBN-10: 1-56647-931-2
ISBN-13: 978-1-56647-931-8
Design by Jane Gillespie
Fourth Printing, June 2012

Library of Congress Cataloging-in-Publication Data

Practice aloha : secrets to living life Hawaiian style : stories, recipes and lyrics from Hawai'i's favorite folks / compiled & edited by Mark Ellman & Barbara Santos with Tehani Kahaialii-Taulava ; photos edited and contributed by Tony Novak-Clifford.
     p. cm.
  ISBN-10: 1-56647-931-2 (softcover : alk. paper)
  ISBN-13: 978-1-56647-931-8
  1. Hawaiians--Social life and customs. 2. Hawaii--Social life and customs. 3. Hawaiian philosophy.
4. Conduct of life. 5. Hawaiian cookery. I. Ellman, Mark. II. Santos, Barbara. III. Kahaialii-Taulava, Tehani.
  DU624.65.P73 2010
  996.9--dc22
                        2010027165

Mutual Publishing, LLC
1215 Center Street, Suite 210
Honolulu, Hawaii 96816
Ph: (808) 732-1709
Fax: (808) 734-4094
e-mail: info@mutualpublishing.com
www.mutualpublishing.com

Printed in Korea

This book is dedicated to the Kanaka Maoli of Hawai'i,
for without them, Aloha would not exist.

And to my wife, Judy,
without her, I would not exist.

Aloha,
Mark Ellman

Contents

PRACTICE ALOHA—THE OLD-STYLE WAY

PRACTICE ALOHA—IN THE KITCHEN

PRACTICE ALOHA—WITH MUSIC

PRACTICE ALOHA—AROUND THE WORLD

PRACTICE ALOHA—ON THE JOB

PRACTICE ALOHA—IN A SPIRITUAL WAY

Acknowledgments

We want to thank the people of Hawai'i who accepted us and taught us what it means to Practice Aloha—without reservation or prejudice. They are the inspiration for this book and our role models every day.

We were astonished and touched by all the people who took the time to write down their memories and thoughts, and we are honored to share their stories of aloha with you. Many of those stories are in this edition, but there are many more—and some amazing video messages—on the Practice Aloha website at www.PracticeAloha.org. Mahalo for sharing.

We could not have created this book without the support and love of our spouses, friends, and extended 'ohana: Jane Gillespie at Mutual Publishing; Laurie McLean, the editor of our edits; and the patrons and staff of the Māla restaurants who showed us that it was time to turn the words "Practice Aloha" into this book.

As a way of sharing our aloha, a good portion of the profits from this book will go toward the Pūnana Leo O Maui, a preschool Hawaiian culture and language immersion program. As the Hawaiian proverb says: *Plan for a year—plant taro. Plan for ten years—plant koa. Plan for one hundred years—teach the children.*

Finally, how can we thank the Spirit of Aloha? Without it, these stories and this book would not have been possible! We hope this book leaves you inspired to live a life guided by aloha.

Mahalo nui loa,
Mark Ellman and Barbara Santos

Foreword

2,500 Years of Practicing Aloha

Two thousand five hundred years ago, a man called Lao Tzu offered us one of the wisest books ever written. It is called the *Tao Te Ching* or the *Book of Living the Virtues of the Great Way.* In this ancient tome, Lao Tzu laid out the four cardinal virtues:

The first cardinal virtue is to have *reverence for all of life.* This means to treat all of God's creatures with love and respect and to look for the unfolding of God in every being, rather than judging or diminishing other beings.

The second cardinal virtue is *natural sincerity,* which manifests as honesty, simplicity and faithfulness. This is the call to make truth your most important attribute and to always practice walking your talk.

The third cardinal virtue is *gentleness*, which manifests itself in consideration for others and spiritual awareness. To Practice Aloha keep this uppermost in mind: "When you have a choice to be right or to be kind, always pick kind."

The fourth cardinal virtue is *supportiveness,* which manifests as service and giving. Here, one lets go of the ego and rather than thinking "What is in it for me?" one asks, "How may I serve?" As the poet Kahlil Gibran offers, "There are those who give with joy and that joy is their reward."

These four cardinal virtues are a road map to the simple truth of the universe—**which is really a pure definition of how to live one's life by Practicing Aloha!** To Practice Aloha recall what Lao Tzu said: "These four virtues are not an external dogma, but rather a part of your original nature."

To revere all of life, to live with natural sincerity, to practice gentleness, and to be in service to others, is to live and Practice Aloha every day.

Sincerely,
Dr. Wayne W. Dyer

Wayne Dyer, Ph.D. is a speaker and the author of over thirty books. His book, *Excuses Begone,* inspired a PBS television special to air in 2010. When not on a lecture tour, he writes from his home on Maui.

Introduction
Why Practice Aloha?

My life in Hawai'i is filled with aloha.

Once you've been to the Islands, you know "aloha" is the most used (and overused) word here. But please understand this: aloha is taken very seriously by the people of Hawai'i. Just because you speak the word, it does not make you a person of aloha. I've learned you need to feel—and live—aloha in order to begin to understand what it truly means.

Now here I am, a white middle-aged man originally from California, talking about aloha like I am an expert. No way! But I do know I want to live my life with aloha in it.

I admit it. Sometimes I let my old mainland ways get in the way. A few years ago, I got caught up in the frenzy of opening Māla, my newest restaurant in Wailea on Maui. You can't ignore deadlines, budgets, and hundreds of important decisions at a time like that, but that is no excuse. As the days wore on, I was finding myself not living up to what I expected of my employees.

Like any business, our restaurants have a mission statement phrase. Ours is "Practice Aloha." How could I forget? It was right there on our Māla bumper stickers and logo T-shirts. That's when I realized, more than ever, I needed to practice what I preached.

For me, placing the words "Practice Aloha" on our wait staff's uniforms was an in-your-face reminder that we must all do our best to be kind and fair and compassionate. The message has caught on in ways I never expected. You can see Practice Aloha bumper stickers on diesel trucks in Minnesota and convertibles in Arizona. People everywhere are beginning to understand and embrace what the words mean.

The last few years have been challenging, haven't they? We need more than ever to Practice Aloha and do whatever we can to make this world a better place for our children and our children's children.

The most beautiful people in the world live in this land of aloha. I can't begin to explain what aloha is, but many of my friends have shared stories with me. Read them and take what is true. Then please share the feeling of aloha with as many people as possible.

Mark Ellman

Aloha: It's the Law

When you move to a new place, there are always things that will surprise you or seem a bit out of the ordinary. Sometimes, however, you happen upon something astounding in your new neighborhood. You realize the folks next door—and just about everyone else for that matter—are acting under the influence of some powerful stuff. Something that makes them want to smile at you for no reason at all! That's what happened when I moved to Hawai'i over twenty years ago.

Did you know having and extending the Aloha Spirit is state law in Hawai'i? Now, I'm not suggesting that is the reason folks are so wonderful here, but it truly is the law:

Hawaii Revised Statutes.
[§5-7.5] The Aloha Spirit:
"Aloha Spirit". (a) "Aloha Spirit" is the coordination of mind and heart within each person. It brings each person to the self. Each person must think and emote good feelings to others. In the contemplation and presence of the life force, "Aloha", the following unuhi laula loa may be used:
"Akahai", meaning kindness to be expressed with tenderness;
"Lokahi", meaning unity, to be expressed with harmony;
"Oluolu", meaning agreeable, to be expressed with pleasantness;
"Haahaa", meaning humility, to be expressed with modesty;

"Ahonui", meaning patience, to be expressed with perseverance.

These are traits of character that express the charm, warmth and sincerity of Hawaii's people. It was the working philosophy of native Hawaiians and was presented as a gift to the people of Hawai'i. "Aloha" is more than a word of greeting or farewell or a salutation. "Aloha" means mutual regard and affection and extends warmth in caring with no obligation in return. "Aloha" is the essence of relationships in which each person is important to every other person for collective existence.

"Aloha" means to hear what is not said, to see what cannot be seen and to know the unknowable.
  (b) In exercising their power on behalf of the people and in fulfillment of their responsibilities, obligations and service to the people, the legislature, governor, lieutenant governor, executive officers of each department, the chief justice, associate justices, and judges of the appellate, circuit, and district courts may contemplate and reside with the life force and give consideration to the "Aloha Spirit".

Even though there is no fine or jail time for infractions of the Aloha Spirit law, it does take aloha to a whole new level!

If you are a visitor to Hawai'i, there's probably a lot you don't know about aloha. So you might want to go slow, read the stories in this book, and give it some contemplation.

Our website, www.PracticeAloha.org, is a central gathering place for folks to tell us what it means to Practice Aloha. Please visit it and add your thoughts. The point isn't to come up with a definitive answer of what aloha is, because the elders have already told us it is beyond our words. (Like a kiss, aloha is better experienced than described!)

But we hope the stories, recipes, and songs shared in this book and on the website will have you living life with lots more of what makes Hawai'i so special: aloha. The best thing we can all do is practice, practice, and practice.

Barbara Santos

Practice Aloha
Every Day

The folks in this chapter clearly know how to appreciate the world around them. They live life with aloha and you can, too!

Some of their stories are funny, while others are a bit more "instructional" in tone. But all are meant to encourage the reader to Practice Aloha in a style that feels right every day.

These stories will remind us to stop and smell the plumeria.

Mark's "Practice Aloha" Story

Mark Ellman

Being in Hawai'i was my destiny. I am where I am supposed to be and my life is filled with good friends, a loving family, and plenty of aloha. But how did I get here?

Looking back, I always said Judy Ellman is responsible for all of that good fortune. Judy lived in Maui in the late 1970s and worked upcountry at the Silversword Inn. But she was drawn back to the mainland to meet her destiny. That would be me: Mark Ellman.

We met in 1977 in Los Angeles, but by 1983 we were ready for a move. Judy told me I'd love living on Maui. Yes, we are here because of my wife and I thank her every day for that.

But the full story is more complex, as things usually are in Hawai'i.

My father died when I was twenty years old. He went in his sleep, unexpectedly—well, at least I wasn't expecting it. I was lost. There were so many questions I never got the chance to ask him. We buried him in Hollywood. My grandmother put "Aloha My Love" on his plaque. Then she took me and my two sisters to Honolulu to see the place my father loved so much.

My dad had been stationed at Schofield Barracks Army Base in the early 1950s. I thought I'd heard all the stories. He was stationed up in the beautiful mountains on the island of O'ahu. My grandmother went to visit him in his Hawai'i military home. As far back as I can remember, when my father and grandmother spoke of the beauty of Hawai'i, they actually called it God's Paradise. My father, Mickey, dreamed of moving to Hawai'i to open a small restaurant and enjoy the year-round beautiful weather, the slow pace, the warm Pacific Ocean, and the aloha of the Hawaiian people he had met there.

I never thought much about Hawai'i while I was in my teens. My free time was consumed with dating girls, making money, smoking pot, and having fun. I never thought much about why my parents got a divorce when I was twelve years old, either. They just did not get along.

Dad became a wholesale meat salesman who sold to restaurants for a living. Sometimes he would take me to work with him. I loved standing in the icy cold walk-in refrigerator smelling the chilled raw meat packaged in cardboard boxes. It's a distinct smell—oddly full of freshness—that is still in my memory. The best part was stealing a cooked knockwurst out of an open box and eating it cold as a snack.

My dad is the one responsible for my career. I never thought of that until now. He got me a weekend job at Texas Tommy's Hamburger Stand in Canoga Park, Los Angeles. I was the weekend janitor. I mopped the floors, cleaned out the trash cans, and swept the parking lot. One day the owner, Chuck, asked me if I was interested in being a cook. I was thirteen years old, just had my Bar Mitzvah, and I was now a man. Why not? My cooking education started with grilled onions, fried burritos, French fries, and the Gold Star Cheeseburger.

I still remember this guy came up to Texas Tommy's one afternoon, obviously a first timer. It was 1968 and McDonald's was serving their millions of burgers at very cheap prices. Texas Tommy's was not McDonald's. We charged a little more, but gave more, too. Our burgers were fantastic. The customer wanted to know why we charged so much for a burger. I explained we used a lot more meat, chili, grilled onions, a smoky beef link—and we butter-grilled our buns. I said, "If you do not like our burger, I will refund your money." I went back to my grill and made sure his burger was perfect. I cooked the onions, sliced new tomatoes and made sure his bun was golden brown. I was not going to lose this offer. I put my soul into this one burger that only the customer and I would ever know about.

Mark's dad, Mickey Ellman, circa late 1960s

He became a regular customer ordering the Gold Star Cheeseburger. To this day I still remember that man's face as he regularly thanked me for a great meal. I was so proud I made a new customer for Texas Tommy's. I put some extra effort and saw amazing results—and I made a connection with my customer. I try and live by that mantra every day of my life. The great part is that in Hawai'i, most people actually notice when you connect with them.

After my first trip to Honolulu back in 1975, I sent out some letters to restaurants and hotels to see how the prospects for work might be. That's when I received my first reply letter signed "Aloha." I was so happy to read that word. Someone wrote me a letter and said "aloha" to me! I felt this strange sense of belonging there, even though I was in Los Angeles.

I have an old photo of my dad standing by himself in front of the Pioneer Inn in Lahaina on Maui. It is a little spooky that today I live about a mile away from where that picture was taken. Was he directing me to come to Maui? All I know is that I have been here for over twenty-five years and he is still talking to me.

Mark Ellman is the driving force behind the Practice Aloha Project. He is best known as a restaurateur and an award-winning chef. He is the author of two cookbooks.

My Aloha Moment

Barbara Santos

I had my first taste of aloha in the Lahaina Foodland supermarket back in 1984. That was twenty-five years ago, yet I still remember it so clearly. The woman involved probably has no idea that I remember our encounter at all. It was just a Tuesday afternoon at work for her....

My extremely tolerant husband, two hungry teenaged sons, one wide-eyed daughter, and I were typical mainland tourists on that trip. We were trying to buy a bit of relaxation in order to reconnect with each other. Ironically we were going to accomplish it all—the relaxing and reconnecting—by booking a jam-packed, seven-day vacation to Maui.

The first thing that bewildered me was the painfully slow pace of the locals. Richard and the kids had already adapted to the leisurely tempo of the island from the moment we boarded the plane in San Francisco. They were so easily sucked in by the complimentary juice and gentle Hawaiian music provided by the airlines.

I wasn't ready to feel the aloha just yet. As we flew over Maui, I kept saying to myself "Let's get this vacation started." Yes, I admit it. I had figured exactly how much—per minute—this vacation was costing us.

From the moment we landed at the old Kahului airport, we simply had too many activities planned. I had convinced Richard we could watch the sunrise on Haleakalā and then drive to Hāna (on the same day, of course). We would find time to hike in ʻĪao Valley, learn to surf, take in a free hula show, and shop for souvenirs at the Lahaina Cannery Mall. We booked an excursion to see the whales. Maybe we would even do a lūʻau. I read through the tourist publications and clipped coupons for even more activities while we waited for our suitcases. Where the hell were they anyway? I was clearly still on Mainland Time, not Maui Time.

The Honoapiʻilani Highway was the only viable route from the airport to the Lahaina side of the island where our vacation condo on the beach awaited. Let me tell you, that road is much longer than a visitor expects. The island looks so small on the maps in *This Week Maui* magazine. How could it possibly take over an hour to get to the hotel? We soon realized the Honoapiʻilani Highway bears no resemblance to a California highway! Twisty and narrow, it hung dangerously close to the edge of seacliffs. The posted speed was fifty-five miles an hour, but we averaged about thirty miles an hour. We were way behind schedule by the time we pulled into Lahaina Town.

"We've got to get snacks for the kids, milk for my tea … oh, some suntan lotion that smells like a piña colada. What do you need?" I asked Rich as he drove our rental car into the Foodland parking lot. He found a spot in the shade of a giant monkeypod tree and parked.

"All I need is to get out of these jeans," he replied. Sweat beads on his forehead were beginning to run down his face.

We all welcomed the blast of air conditioning as the Foodland doors slid open for us. The store seemed similar to a mainland supermarket—until we got inside. The store's loudspeakers were playing slack-key guitar music and the perfume of tuberose flowers wafted toward us from the lei display at the store entrance.

We didn't know a papaya from a mango. There were tubs of florescent colored "stuff" in the deli case alongside the blocks of fresh tofu wrapped in damp pink paper. The fish counter held unusual seafood with unfamiliar names, tiny octopi and blue crabs, lomilomi salmon, and at least a half-dozen types of poke—raw fish cubes laced with shoyu (soy sauce), green onions, seaweed, and sesame seeds. We filled up a cart with both kitchen staples and exotic foods to try … but I remember I talked the kids out of breakfast cereal because $5 a box for Kellogg's Froot Loops seemed outrageous and totally unnecessary with so many new foods to try.

Nearly forty-five minutes later we rolled our shopping cart to the checkout stand. The clerk, a middle-aged woman with an enormous pink flower behind her ear, smiled at us and said "Aloha." So people actually did say "aloha" beyond the airport limits. I had speculated it was only a marketing ploy for the tourists. The checkout lady began clicking away on the cash register keyboard.

"Mom, how does that flower stay in her hair?" my daughter whispered to me. Actually, we were both curious. It looked amazing against her shiny black hair. The woman noticed we were staring at her head. She stopped, took the flower from her hair and began to dismantle it.

"See, it's really lots of plumeria blossoms. You put one on top of the other and it makes one big flower. You would wear it over your right ear, but your mom would wear it on the left side because she is 'taken,'" the woman told my daughter.

Well, that was interesting, but what was this woman thinking? She was talking to us like we had all afternoon when there were PEOPLE IN LINE BEHIND US!!!!

She reassembled the flower, put it back over her ear and continued clicking the register keys. "Auwē, you got lomilomi salmon but no sweet bread?" She looked at us like we had so much to learn about Island cuisine. She tossed back her head and her eyes focused on an end-aisle display of King's Bakery breads a few feet away. Richard bounded over and grabbed a loaf of Portuguese sweet bread while the woman waited … along with the people behind us in line.

The woman and Richard chatted as they bagged our groceries at the far end of the counter, while I fumbled to find some cash. Was it in my purse, or still in my carry-on bag back in the car? What time did we need to check into the hotel? Oh no, we forgot the suntan lotion! I checked my watch: HURRY, HURRY, HURRY!

The woman walked back to the cash register and I extended my hand with the cash. She didn't sweep up the bills with the minimal human contact of a mainland clerk. She held my hand, looked me in the eyes and said, "Slow down." It wasn't a command. It wasn't a reprimand. It was simply the truth.

She held my hand until I felt the tension in my shoulders melting away. It was only a few moments but I can still feel her touch and hear her voice. She was someone who saw I was driving down the highway of life much too fast. I was missing the best part of the journey by watching the speedometer and dashboard clock instead of rolling down the windows and taking in all the beauty along the way. I wouldn't believe it either, but all I can tell you is that I listened to her and it changed me.

Back in the car, I couldn't explain what had just happened. Was she my guardian angel? No, she was simply a woman who Practiced Aloha and shared it with me that afternoon. I wanted to take her with me everywhere for the rest of my life. Funny thing is, in a way, I still do.

Now when my life gets too frantic and filled with deadlines, I close my eyes and remember the checkout lady from Foodland in Lahaina. Then I slow down, call a friend, and, sometimes, I even go outside and pick some pink flowers for my desk.

Barbara is an author and marketing/public relations professional. She lived on Maui for fifteen years, returned to the San Francisco Bay Area (where she is marketing director for the San Francisco Writers Conference), but returns home to Maui frequently.

Aloha Style

Helen Hunt

We have an expression in our house … with our daughter … when we're rushing anywhere …
When we're getting too worked up about anything we say,

"Let's do it, aloha style."

Aloha style means:

Slowly, gently,
with peace in our hearts,
softly, with love …

Helen Hunt is best known for playing Jaime on *Mad About You* and for winning an Oscar for *As Good As It Gets*. Helen and her family come to Maui frequently for quality time and a bit of "decompressing" between movies and television shows.

In Hawai'i there is an unwritten understanding that celebrities and their families are treated with respect and privacy, just as any other visitor would be. Helen, and so many other show business personalities, know an escape to the Island lifestyle restores all that is truly important in life.

Pratice Makes Perfect

Shep Gordon & Renee Loux Gordon

Aloha is the generous spirit of the Islands. It is the intangible, yet ever-present magic woven into the wind, the earth, the waters, and the heartstrings of anyone who has had the fortune to land on the shores of the magnificent Hawaiian archipelago.

The meaning of aloha is evasive, yet unmistakable. This one word embodies the embrace of the Islands and her people—the call of the conch at the blaze of sunset, the rustle of palm fronds in the tradewinds, the haunting beauty of the whale's song, the rush of surf on velvet sand, the reign of waterfalls through ancient valleys, the seductive scent of flowers, and the arch of a rainbow between worlds where the veils are thin.

Aloha is leaving your slippers at the door, taking the road less traveled, imbibing the warmth of the sweet things in life and letting it hang loose.

Like anything, practice makes perfect and the practice of aloha gets sweeter and deeper the more we embrace it and the more we allow ourselves to be embraced by it.

When celebrities come to Maui, they stop by to see Shep and Renee. Shep has produced movies (Kiss of the Spider Woman) and created Alive Films, the first independent film production company in the U.S. His Alive Culinary Resources represented renowned chefs like Emeril Lagasse and Alice Waters.

Renee is an actress, chef, and host of the television show *It's Easy Being Green*. She moved to Maui in 1995 and soon opened one of America's first raw foods restaurants, *The Raw Experience*. Renee is the author of two cookbooks and starred with Woody Harrelson in the film *Go Further*.

Use Your Voice of Aloha

Richard Rutherford

I have been most fortunate to have lived in Hawaii for the past ten years and I have found it is a much greater feeling to "Practice Aloha" then to receive it. "Aloha" has many, many definitions. Hello and good-bye, love, compassion, mercy, kindness, grace, sweetheart, lover, loved one…Wow!

Each and every day we all have the opportunity to "Practice Aloha". When you personally experience aloha, and you conform to the aloha spirit as I have, it is so much easier to "Practice Aloha".

By helping others while practicing aloha, you have the opportunity to use the "voice of aloha" to shout out your enthusiasm for life here in Hawaii. Aloha, Aloha, Aloha!

Richard retired from the active world of business and moved to Hawaii in 1998 at age 62. He gets to 'Practice Aloha' every day, so he is now 45 years old!

Aloha is a Kiss

Brad Liko Rogers

As I thought about the word "aloha" and what it meant to me, I thought about a very special kupuna: Tūtū Lydia Hale.

I was going to school at U.H. Mānoa. While sitting in her office, Tūtū explained what she felt was the source of the word "aloha." Kupuna Hale said that "aloha" is two Hawaiian words combined. "Alo," the face of a person and "ha," breathing in the air of life through the nose.

According to Tūtū Hale, two people kissing, face-to-face in the Hawaiian fashion, sharing a single breath of life, is where the word "aloha" comes from. I truly appreciate Tūtū Hale's sharing this meaning with me.

In Hawaiian

I koʻu noʻonoʻo ʻana i ka hua ʻōlelo "aloha" a me kona manaʻo iaʻu, Haliʻa aʻela au i kahi kupuna makamae loa. ʻO Tūtū Lydia Hale kona inoa. I koʻu wā e hele ana i ke kulanui o Hawaiʻi ma Mānoa, aia nō kēia e noho ana ma kona keʻena ma laila. Wehewehe maila ʻo Tūtū i kona manaʻo no ke kumu o ka hua ʻōlelo "aloha." ʻĪ maila ʻo Kupuna Hale, ʻo ke "aloha" he ʻelua hua ʻōlelo Hawaiʻi i hoʻohui ʻia i hoʻokahi. ʻo "alo," ʻo ia hoʻi ka helehelena o kekahi kanaka, a ʻo "hā", ka hanu ʻana i ke ea o ke ola ma ka ihu. Wahi a Tūtū Hale ʻo ka honi ʻana o ʻelua kanaka alo a he alo ma ke ʻano Hawaiʻi a me ka hanu pū ʻana i ia hā hoʻokahi, no laila mai ka hua ʻōlelo "aloha." Mahalo nui loa au iā Tūtū Hale i kona kaʻanalike ʻana i ia manaʻo me aʻu.

Brad is a Hawaiian language teacher who lives on Maui. He wrote the Hawaiian blessing for this book.

Unzipping the Aloha

Debra Casey

I updated my Facebook status saying that I was trying to come up with what the Aloha Spirit meant to me. My friend Nathaniel wrote back with this: "Letting strangers crash on your floor and taking them to surf the amazing waves of Maui!!"

I met Nathaniel in Huntington Beach when I was trying to get out of my wetsuit and I needed help. I live and surf on Maui and had never worn a wetsuit before. I was stuck.

Well, he helped me out, so I gave him my card and said, "If you are ever on Maui ..."

Now he is a good friend who I would welcome in my home any time. I think being open to making new real friends encompasses the Aloha Spirit for me.

Debra is an actress, vegan, surfer, and body piercer at Atomic Tattoo in Lahaina.

Mutual Aloha

Chris Kaiwi

Aloha means caring and treating someone the way that you would like to be cared for or treated … and doing it with a smile that is genuine and sincere.

Chris is vice president and managing partner of the Pineapple Grill at Kapalua Resort.

More Than a Word

Ray Masters

A loha is much, much more than just a word.
It is the free spirit within me (my inner child), heart and soul, manifested by thinking good thoughts, emoting good feelings, and sharing goodness with others.

It embodies kindness, tenderness, and being unassuming.

There is harmony in aloha, but in reality aloha is ineffable: there are no words to describe it.

Just like sunrise on Haleakalā or a swim in the ʻĪao Stream, aloha has to be experienced—indeed, felt—to be understood.

Ray is a commercial artist designing posters for major sporting events and a successful fine artist, as well. He lives in a beach house on Maui with his windsurfing gear ready at all times.

Aloha Means…

Richard Donner and Lauren Shuler Donner

To us, aloha means home.

The Donners are film directors and producers of blockbuster movies including *The Omen* and *Superman* (Richard) and *Mr. Mom* and *X-Men* (Lauren). They have premiered several of their movies in Hawaiʻi as fundraisers for the Maui Humane Society.

Aloha is the Beautiful Sea

Angel Melody Bode

I grew up on Maui, born and raised. To me, aloha means having consideration for the land. Aloha is the beautiful sea with its dolphins, whales, and turtles. It's nature, like the pretty flowers and plants. They smile back and only give beauty to make every day an amazing day.

Aloha is being friendly and the friendly people who smile back at you.

Aloha is hugs and kisses, love, and warmth.

Angel is a surfer and an artist known on Maui for painting large murals including one at Lahainaluna High School. She recently illustrated her first children's book, Kalani's Wish.

See Aloha in Yourself

Dennis Blevins

All practice of aloha is done from the kindness of our hearts, no other reason. Aloha is always with you; it is a part of you. It's not something you put on and take off.

A simple act of aloha can be holding a door open for someone you don't know, as you smile and say, "Aloha."

Then you have the ultimate act of aloha. "No greater gift has man as to give his life for a friend." Our troops do this on a daily basis and they don't even know us.

Aloha is alive and well. If you don't see the aloha, then you are not Practicing Aloha. You see the aloha in yourself.

This story was submitted via the Practice Aloha website www. PracticeAloha.org.

Aloha is Unconditional

Tehani Kahaialii-Taulava

Aloha to me is unconditional; it is many things put together.

Aloha is when you …

… see a familiar face and your heart is filled with joy and excitement even if you had seen that person only yesterday.

… sit with a friend, old or new, and talk story.

… pass a stranger on the street and smile—just because.

… help someone you see is in need of it.

… say you're sorry for bumping into someone in the store.

… let a car cut in front of you with out beeping your horn.

… say please and thank you.

… excuse yourself to answer a phone call.

… share your bento or plate lunch with a friend.

… love and respect your family, friends, and even complete strangers.

All of these things are what aloha means to me.

Living and Practicing Aloha is not an obligation; it's a way of life. Share aloha, respect aloha, live aloha.

Tehani is the project coordinator for Practice Aloha. We can verify she is a delight to have on the team and she genuinely practices what she shares in this prose/poem she wrote.

Ambassadors of Aloha

Chaney Countryman

Though I was born on Maui and lived my entire life on this island paradise, I've only begun to understand a small part of what ancient Hawaiians called "aloha" and its profound daily effect on my life. Aloha is not just a word or thought, but a path we choose to walk. It is the attempt to make the life of everyone we meet a little bit better, because our paths have crossed and we have "touched" them. Aloha is an attitude toward life and those who share that life.

Aloha is an awareness of what and who is around you—the opposite of self-centeredness. Aloha might mean something as simple as smiling at a passerby, jumping in the ocean, or sharing a meal with a friend in need. It's a show of gratitude for the abundance and beauty that surrounds us.

Aloha is powerful and sometimes its energy can give me chicken skin! Aloha is a choice; to see the good, to treat each other, our 'āina, and our makai with genuine respect. Maui is but one small island with everyone dependent—to a greater or lesser degree—on the welfare of others. Awareness and regard for others and our surroundings are the essence of living aloha—a gift to all from the island's host culture.

Practicing Aloha is a gift that elevates us to a higher rhythm of life. We must all be ambassadors of aloha!

Bill and Chaney Countryman are father and daughter. Chaney is an outstanding student at Lahainaluna High School. Bill is the general manager of the Wailea Beach Marriott Resort and Spa.

A Foundation of Aloha

Susan Moulton

I believe we are all born with Aloha Spirit. But bumps in the road in our lives lead us as adults to forget all of the warm, loving feelings we are born with.

I realized something profound when I lost my youngest son, Will, when he was eight. He was the person he was because he had received so much positive influence in his short life. He received it, and he spread it. He had no problem giving aloha and a smile.

This idea spilled out from my broken heart—a foundation to create and support positive life experiences for children all over the world! Let's see if we cannot become happier, more loving adults as a result of our acts of kindness and generosity.

It is a daunting task in today's world, but if we look to our children, cherish their innocence, and take the time to really enjoy those smiles, perhaps it will become easier to spread those smiles—and spread aloha.

Susan created the Will Smith Foundation as a memorial to her young son, who died in a traffic accident on Maui. The foundation has donated thousands of dollars to projects in Hawai'i and around the world.

Nikilani and Jade

Toni Rojas

I write this for my daughter, Nikilani, who is thirteen years old with special needs. Some of us are born with aloha and some of us learn aloha. Nikilani was born with the genuine and heartfelt Spirit of Aloha.

Every day in every way, she shows passion for life and every person in it. She believes we should all work and play together, share together, and help each other any way we possibly can. We are all family and we are all friends, as we are all in this together as one. She just can't imagine why any one would think otherwise.

She sees no boundaries. No matter what physical or mental limitations we might have, as far as she is concerned, there are no limitations. The sky is the limit!

Recently when Nikilani met Mark and Judy Ellman at a chef's festival, she was determined to help them at their booth. How can I thank them for embracing her and practicing what they preach? They did Practice Aloha that day. A photo of all of them together is now up in her room as an inspiration!

Each night, as we wind down our day, I ask her what were the three most wonderful things she experienced in her day. She never is able to keep the list to three and always makes sure that Molly, her social-therapy dog and her older seventeen-year-old sister and idol, Jade, are at the top of the list.

The beauty of her innocence is inspiring to us as parents and she truly touches those around her with her love of life. We think she is an unofficial teen ambassador of Practicing Aloha, and we couldn't be prouder.

Toni is one proud mom. She says Nikilani's dream is to become a renowned Maui chef and has already set her sights on the MCC Culinary Academy.

Say Aloha First Thing in the Morning

Patrick Ching

I look forward to my first chance of the day to share aloha. Many of my neighbors have stress. I have stress. When we smile and say aloha in the morning it sets the tone for a day of love ahead. When someone receives aloha, they can't wait to share it.

Patrick is a wildlife artist, rodeo clown, and author of children's coloring books. He lives in Waimānalo and has galleries on O'ahu and Kaua'i.

Aloha, State of Grace

Georja Skinner

Flashback to Lahaina, 1980, when my now ex-husband Paul and I took a leap of faith and moved to Maui. We moved away from our friends and family in Hollywood and I left behind a successful career as a sound mixer in television.

The decision was based on the promise of new horizons. I felt connected to this place. The land was alive. The spirit of ancient rhythms in the breezes, in the music, in the dance that communicated the essence of Hawai'i both past and present—all of it spoke to me on a cellular level. It is the very reason I have called Hawai'i home for twenty-nine years, or, as we used to say, "We're on the twenty-ninth year of our three-week vacation!"

Yes, just two weeks after Paul and I arrived, we made a decision to stay and rented a condo in Wailea. I traded in an established career for the vast unknown of this new land. I felt alive and renewed.

But without warning, just three weeks after I arrived, I lost the sense of taste in my mouth and shortly thereafter, I awoke to my face frozen on the left side. Then my left eye and mouth. In fact the entire left side of my face was paralyzed.

A bit startling in contrast to the serenity that surrounded me. I rushed to a doctor who diagnosed me with Bell's Palsy. "Not sure what causes it, either a virus or a freezing of the facial nerves. Sometimes it's brought on by stress."

Stress? I was living in paradise; how could that possibly be stressful? But indeed, I had unfinished business that only the island and its innate healing powers could teach me.

"No swimming, stay off the beach, and tape your eye shut at night so you won't scratch your cornea." Lovely. All this time dreaming of living and working here in Maui, why now? Instead of swimming in

Maui's glorious waters, I was forced to look at the landscape like a picture postcard as the months ticked by.

For the next six months, I watched the sun rise and set from my condo lanai, heard stories of progress and adventure about the sailing charter boat we bought and were running. And still no movement.

How I longed to find out "why" and get my face to smile again. Marx Brothers movies, bringing my old show, *The Jeffersons,* to Oʻahu—none of it made a difference. The face was still frozen. I adapted somewhat, finding humor in the whole situation, wearing the eye patch from a kid's pirate kit I found at the Longs in Kahului. Could I wear it to the beach? ARRGH!

I don't know what possessed me to do it but at month six I had had enough. I was determined to go in the water. I would be careful, I promised the doctor. I just wanted to feel the breeze in my hair and be enveloped by the ocean once more.

I went out on our charter boat, the *Scotch Mist,* that morning with my husband Paul and a few passengers. I was moved to tears by the power of the air, the wind, the sea. I sensed they were drawing me to a soothing, welcoming safe harbor at last. I recalled how far I had come from the madness of my job as a sound mixer in Hollywood, and how the rhythm of this place was much more aligned with my own spirit.

It was then that a voice said to me, "Come in." It was beckoning me back home. After we anchored the boat in Lahaina Harbor and said our alohas to our fellow "sailors," I asked Paul to stop at Launiupoko Park on our way back to Wailea so I could take that careful plunge.

I wandered out on the beach and eased into the warm Maui ocean. I ran my hands in the deep sand and gently massaged Mother Nature into my immobilized face, all the while praying for healing.

It seemed like forever that I was there. Paul was kind enough to let me be. When I got back to the car I felt whole again. The ocean had kissed me.

The next morning, after showering, I recalled the wonder of the experience. It brought a smile to my heart and a deep sense of grace. Just being in the water renewed me. I looked at my reflection in the mirror and saw my frozen face had re-awakened. Mother Maui had brought me back together again.

The six-month journey had taught me to listen to that voice inside and to the voices of nature that surround us. There is divine order in life. For me, finding and connecting with the spirit of this land where I live meant I had finally found "home." Through this experience, the spirit of these islands taught me to live with that Spirit of Aloha, to practice the grace and humility of this land and her people. For this, I am forever grateful.

Georja is an author and works in the Creative Industries Division of the Hawai'i Department of Business, Economic Development and Tourism.

The Gift of Hula

Aunty Kahana (Debra First)

My experience when I dance hula is always a blessing to me ...

I had been dancing for many years when I had a stroke ten years ago. I went back to a beginner's class for what I thought would be just physical therapy. It was much more.

My mind, body and spirit came back to me! Now, when I dance, I am transformed, whether in front of an audience or just in practice (which I personally enjoy more).

This story was submitted via the Practice Aloha website. www.PracticeAloha. org

A Revelation of Aloha

Taken from a transcript of a recording of Moe Keale

In her "Aloha Chant" Hawai'i's beloved spiritual teacher, Pilahi Paki, explained that the infinite Divine Love embodied in the word "Aloha" is to be shared with all people. In a revelation she received in the early 1970s, Auntie Pilahi was told that the islands of Hawai'i would play a pivotal role in the history of the world. She said because of the turmoil that would arise in world in the 21st century, nations would look to the loving spirit of Hawai'i because Hawai'i's "Aloha" holds the key to world peace.

In a concert at the Hawai'i Theater, Moe Keale, Hawai'i's legendary singer, shared with the audience his remembrance of Pilahi Paki's prophetic words. "In the year, 2000, Auntie Pilahi said that the world is going to be in a lot of trouble. She said when that happens, there are going to be a lot of arguments, a lot of misunderstandings, it's going to turn into fighting, and it's going to turn into fighting, and it's going to turn into wars. She said when that happens, the rest of the world will be looking to Hawai'i for help and the reason for that is because Hawai'i has the key to world peace, and that key is "Aloha."

And we who live here, it doesn't matter if we were born or raised here or not, the fact that we are here makes us special, and the reason we are special is because if we are born here, we are born with Aloha.

But if we live here, and we come from outside, and you stay here long enough, you can't help but aloha runs into you, and you're trapped! That's what makes us different."

Moe went on to say, "Now when Pilahi told me that by the year 2000 that this was going to happen, you know, I believed her, and I did. Then, the week after Christmas last year, in 1999, I was invited to go to Kauai for a world peace conference. I went and I shared aloha with them, and as I was doing it, I realized that these guys were the first ones. They're the start. They're coming, you know. They're coming to Hawai'i to look for whatever it is they're looking for and I know what it is, it's ALOHA."

Pilahi Paki passed away in 1985 and Moe Keale in 2002. We encourage you to learn more about these amazing Hawaiian leaders who shared the universal concepts of aloha with the world.

Aloha is Unconditional Love

Jodee Haugh

Aloha is the practice of positive communication and fostering harmony and peace in all relationships. Aloha is having a person-centered approach in everything that you do and giving your very best to every person that you encounter.

Hawai'i has a culture rooted in compassion and graciousness. Aloha is what makes Hawai'i unique and more than a tourist destination.

Jodee is a professional make-up artist. She is on the production crew for the Big Island Film Office and has created special effects for disaster preparedness films.

Growing Aloha

Cecilia Bahena

I expressed my love of plants to a woman who was waiting along with me at the doctor's office. She asked me where I worked and a few days later she arrived with a small variety of plants for me. She told me that she knew I would care for them and this meant a lot to her because she raised her plants from babies.

I have been very fortunate to experience aloha in many ways during my life. I think of these events of aloha and smile.

This story was submitted via the Practice Aloha website. www.PracticeAloha. org

Essence of Aloha

Hawaiʻi State Senator Roz Baker

If you were arrested for Practicing Aloha, would there be enough evidence to convict? For a group of women in South Maui, the answer is a resounding yes! As part of their contribution to the Relay for Life, they decided to knit more than twenty-five shawls to give to cancer survivors they didn't know—an act of aloha that came from the heart.

To me, the essence of the Aloha Spirit comes from the Hawaiian values embodied in the letters of the word "aloha"— ʻakahai, lōkahi, ʻoluʻolu, haʻahaʻa, and ahonui. In English we'd translate these values as kindness, harmony, pleasantness, humility, and patience.

People making a positive difference in another person's life: that's Practicing Aloha.

Roz Baker serves in the Hawaiʻi State Senate and is chair of the Senate Ways and Means Committee. She is a longtime advocate for issues that affect the quality of life such as health care and public education.

Feeling Aloha

Cindy Beadles

The first time I felt the Aloha Spirit, I was stepping off the plane into the open-air airport in Honolulu. The smell of the plumeria trees and flowers from the lei stands brought me to life.

I still feel fully alive, just as I did way back then, when I travel on the windy Hāna Highway. Windows open, arms hanging out. The wet, fragrant, and fermented smells. The canopy of greenery relaxes my mind and brings me pure happiness.

Mahalo to my senses for reminding me to practice feeling aloha!

Cindy is a wife and mother who has lived on Maui for almost thirty years. Originally from Washington State, she has worked with Mark and Judy Ellman since 1991.

Talking About Aloha at the Boys & Girls Club

Students of the Boys & Girls Club of Maui

O ne thing aloha means is when people get together and talk story with each other.

—Malia Kanohokula Age 11

Aloha means love. Aloha means you care about someone. Say aloha to everybody in your family.

—Rench Tubelliza Age 12

Aloha means a polite greeting—as in, "Hello and welcome to the island of Hawai'i."

—Babymae Jano Age 14

What aloha means to me is, "Welcome to this 'āina." It means have a good a time in the world.

—Isaiah Camara Age 13

The word "aloha" means welcome. So every time someone new comes into your life you would say aloha to them. It is also for respect. The word "aloha" means a lot to me and my family.

—Courtney Galarita Age 13

Aloha means to wear some flowers and go catch some tako.

—D. Briley Neyenhuis Age 11

Aloha means taking care of the island. Jarred Arakawa Age 14

What aloha means is to care for one another. A word meant to be said for a starting friendship.
— Sharmaine Guitierrez Age 11

What aloha means to me? Aloha means a lot and I will yell … ALOHA!!!!!!!
— Kaleo Carbajal Age 12

Aloha Is ...

Hawai'i State Senator J. Kalani English

Aloha is being surrounded by those you love,
being at home where you are,
and being mindful of others.

J. Kalani English was raised in Hāna, Maui, by his grandparents, who instilled in him a strong work ethic and a dedication to family and community. Bilingual in English and Hawaiian, he was an advisor for the UN and now serves as an elected Hawai'i lawmaker.

Love and Fear

Matt Smith

My mother taught me from a young age that there are two basic emotions: love and fear. It took me years to realize how true it was. You can either count your blessings and focus on what is going right or dwell on what you lack. Love is open, kind, and grateful. Fear is cloistered and stubborn. They do not co-exist.

Aloha has many meanings but love is its core and substance. Aloha radiates warmth, generosity, and affection. Aloha is a neighborly fondness that is the essence of Hawai'i and its people.

It is a very lofty concept, but it is as simple as a smile. It is the state of mind that serves us best. Aloha is love.

Matt is an artist and the son of another artist: Andrea Smith.

Practice Aloha Secret

Mikel Mesh

Aloha is the first thing I noticed when I moved to Maui in 1979. In fact, aloha seemed to be blooming everywhere back then as the fragrance of kindness mingled in the soft tropical air.

Thirty years later, though the Islands have changed in many ways, the necessity of Practicing Aloha has never been more important. There is a good reason why we live in Hawai'i, and the secret is aloha.

Mikel the artist, at age nine, won the coveted Golden Sharpie Award at the Cartoon Olympics held in Reykjavik, Iceland. (Check out his daily cartoon website: www.DailyFlounder.com.) Today, as publisher of The Best Publishing Co., he produces gorgeous magazines for Hawai'i tourists. He is also a jewelry designer.

Aloha Moments

Jerry Labb

I feel most people, in general, are nice wherever I go on the planet. But here in Hawai'i, I'll get more smiles per mile than anywhere else. It seems people here aren't as afraid to smile and say hello (or aloha) to each other.

In some other places, maybe because of crime or hard times, people are trying to suck your energy or your money from you. So making eye contact is kept at a minimum. But I see the Aloha Spirit everywhere I go in Hawai'i. I see folks greeting and hugging each other with aloha in their hearts and eyes.

One of my favorite "aloha moments" is when two cars stop on the road going in opposite directions and the drivers start to "talk story." No one honks, everyone waits. Then, as we all get going again, everyone flashes the shaka sign!

Jerry is a longtime Maui resident who is active in local charities and arts events.

Living Aloha

Ryan Burden

I've been fortunate enough to live on Maui for seven years now. Though I've only begun to understand a small part of what ancient Hawaiians called aloha, it has had a profound daily effect on my life.

To me the moments of aloha are when we treat each other and the earth with genuine respect and show gratitude for the abundance that surrounds us all. It's when we are truthful, kind, and caring. We Practice Aloha when we choose to see the good everywhere (and thus create more of it). We can feel aloha when we take the time to fill our bodies with healthy, natural foods and appreciate the daily miracle of life on earth.

It's powerful stuff and sometimes I get doses of it so strong it literally gives me goose bumps! So smile, laugh with a friend, jump in the ocean, share a delicious meal, or give to those in need. You'll feel the energy of aloha. Practicing it is healthy and fun ... and eventually it elevates you to a higher rhythm of life.

Ryan is a surfer and a practitioner of aloha! His story was submitted via the Practice Aloha website. www.PracticeAloha.org

Practice Aloha
The Old-Style Way

Ahh, the good old days when life was simpler.

Or was it?

The following stories are filled with warm memories and essential life lessons. Many focus on how the ʻohana—that uniquely Hawaiian concept of family—was the source of great strength in a time of crisis.

The rules for Practicing Aloha haven't changed much. On an island it just makes good sense to share what you can, take only what you need, and respect each other. Wouldn't it be wonderful if the world saw itself as the island it truly is?

Aloha and the Pioneer

Kimo Falconer

"Aloha" and "'ohana" to me are synonymous. I am the progeny of two vastly differing families, both with pioneering backgrounds. That word haunts me—pioneer.

My California lineage goes back to the time of the range wars between the sodbusters, cattlemen, and sheep ranchers. At the same time my 'ohana in Hawai'i was enduring the annexation of the last frontier of the great westward movement. On one hand I have an ancestor listed among the great pioneers of the San Joaquin Valley; on the other, I have the founder of the Pioneer Hotel in Lahaina who was married to a pure Hawaiian.

Ironically, there was also a Pioneer Hotel in my father's hometown of Porterville, California. That's where I spent my youth on the family ranch. I drove tractors, fished for trout, and remember wonderful holiday dinners around a fireplace or giant picnics in the wildflower hills of the Sierras. The aloha ran deep.

In California, I was the dark skinned farm boy with the strange name. (I was named after my father's best buddy, but "James," my mother quickly announced, would be "Kimo.") The Mexican girls liked me, which usually meant I would get my ass kicked. Back on Maui, I spoke poor pidgin, which also meant the same fate. I once tried to make sashimi out of a trout. Bad idea. It was not uncommon to find both poi and tacos on our dinner plates.

First sign of summer each year, my brother and I were on our way to Maui. Upon arrival we were lei'd from head to toe. The smell of those flowers lingers. We were the first to the "board rack" at Lahaina harbor—borrowing surfboards. We ate raw everything, got pāpaʻa skin and played with children of every ethnicity. At every door, there was a sea of rubber footwear. I figure the reason I can wiggle my ears today is because I never stopped laughing as a kid.

I graduated from a nice university in California. I studied and got my degree in agriculture. When it came to job interview time, I got an offer from a Hawaiʻi sugar plantation. The return address on the envelope read "Pioneer Mill Company, Ltd."

Whether coincidence or destiny, I had to take the job.

It all works out, doesn't it? My wife and I are holding on our shoulders two sons who will carry on the legacy, just as we are standing on the shoulders of pioneers. ʻOhana is the source of what aloha means to me. The miracle of how it all came to be.

Kimo, a lifelong farmer, was the Agricultural Research Director for Pioneer Mill Co. for over twenty years. When the mill closed, he started MauiGrown Coffee and opened a retail store in 2006 on the site of the mill. MauiGrown Coffee is the only worldwide producer of 100 percent Maui-origin coffee.

Aloha in Everyday Life

Mayor Charmaine Tavares

As a child growing up on Maui, I learned early on the importance of aloha in everyday life. Neighbors shared their harvest, and friends were always eager to lend a hand. Even complete strangers would not blink an eye at dropping everything they were doing to help someone in need. Taking care of one another wasn't something that was taught in school; it was simply a way of life. It was a natural outpouring of kindness, generosity, and goodwill.

Now that our Islands' population has grown and changed in many ways, it's especially important to continue to Practice Aloha in our community. I am touched by the aloha shared by the many folks I meet and work with each day. The Spirit of Aloha is a gift we can share with others. It is one of the most special things about Maui nei.

As mayor of Maui County, Mayor Tavares has constituents on three islands: Maui, Lāna'i, and Moloka'i. She is known as an advocate for the environment and the use of alternative fuels. She has worked in the public service sector most of her life, following the lead of her father, the late Hannibal Tavares, who was also Maui's mayor for many years.

Fifty Years as the Fiftieth State

Governor Neil Abercrombie

For the better part of ten hours the droning hum of the Pan Am propellers put me in a state of drowsy indifference. Then, suddenly, my childhood dreamscape of Hawai'i—sparked by a chance encounter with a book on the Islands at Public School 63 in Buffalo, NY—was made real.

There it was: Pearl Harbor, the graceful curve of O'ahu's shoreline, and Diamond Head. The whirring of the engines sputtered to a halt, a portable stairway was wheeled up and then—gently, delightfully—I felt the warmth of the sun and a fresh breeze.

A quick stop at the Short Snorter Bar on the edge of the tarmac, and then I was in the car of Professor Glick and driving toward Mānoa Valley, the University of Hawai'i, and the teaching assistantship in sociology that awaited me.

In Chinatown, at the corner of Smith and King streets, I saw the most handsome man I'd ever seen: thick mane of white hair, bronzed, clear-eyed, square-jawed, with a frame exuding vitality and purpose. Any place that produces such a person, I thought, must have qualities of life and properties of culture I'd never experienced anywhere on the East Coast.

But the world he represented was about to change forever. Two weeks before—in the wake of Nisei soldiers returning from World War II, the tsunami of Democratic victories in the 1954 Territorial Legislature and the election of working-class favorite John Burns to the U.S. Congress—Hawai'i had become a state. The air was full of optimism and confidence; statehood was something almost everybody wanted because it represented equality and opportunity. Statehood also represented modernity and change meant to spur progress. Fifty years ago, no one knew what that change would look like: The jet planes and mainland millionaires had not arrived, and the U.S. military had not morphed into a Pacific Command astride all of Asia. The world I entered was still the world of the Waikīkī beach boys and Hawaii Calls. The Legislature met in a palace. The Columbia Inn served oxtail soup twenty-four hours a day. King Street ran two ways. Traffic lights were few. And cows grazed on the Mānoa campus I was bound for.

Once settled at the professor's hillside home just off O'ahu Avenue, I couldn't sleep. I wandered with the creeping darkness toward the university and beyond, marveling at the stars. I felt I'd never known what the heavens actually were until then.

My reverie was halted as I approached the junction of University Avenue and Beretania and King streets. Just up from the intersection was a sign: Paris Café. I had to investigate.

Inside it was nondescript. I walked up to the small bar at the rear—a newly minted graduate of Union College in Schenectady, all brush cut and Bermuda shorts—and sat on a stool to the right of several men. Conversation stopped, followed by small smiles and stares. I announced I'd just arrived to teach at the university and would appreciate an introduction to Hawai'i and the neighborhood. The smiles broadened, and hands were extended and shaken.

"Aloha, brah."

"Your first day, fo' real?"

"New York, fo' real?"

The bartender said what I needed was to experience a little local culture and that I'd come to the right place.

"You have to try some pūpūs. You drink, you eat local style. You ever try chopsticks?"

A dish of what seemed to be salad appeared in front of me. Instructions on chopstick protocol were issued. A bottle of Royal Beer—"drink local, bruddah"—materialized. Awkwardly, I grasped the chopsticks and decided the better part of honor required me to use them shovel-like to heave a huge portion into my mouth. Kim chee!

I watched faces light up as I desperately tried to swallow as fast as I could. I grabbed for the beer. Let's just say the flavor of the Royal was unique. "Royal Beer—right from the Ala Wai to you, brah." Somehow, I choked it all down, teary-eyed and trying not to gasp. By now everyone was standing and applauding.

"Welcome to Hawai'i."

"Good job!"

"Aloha."

That world too has all but disappeared. Not just the Paris Café, but the Kuhio Grill, the Denver Grill, CoCo's, the Tahitian Lanai and, of course, the Columbia Inn. Roy's, Alan Wong's, even Sam Choy's are not the same thing. They're not even close.

As the fiftieth anniversary of statehood approaches, I am filled with nostalgia for the place that embraced me when I arrived as a young man—and also with a sense of the irony inherent in statehood: Yes, Hawai'i wanted the change that statehood has brought, but we also wanted everything to stay as it was. That is, what we really wanted was for everything to change but us.

Neil Abercrombie served as Hawai'i's representative to the U.S. Congress for nineteen years. This story originally appeared in *Hana Hou!*, the inflight magazine for Hawaiian Airlines.

Aloha at the Hawaiiana Club

Jan Kitaguchi

Aloha that came from the heart was the legacy of Uncle Jimmie Greig, the director and co-founder of the Lahainaluna High School's Boarders' Chorus and Hawaiiana Club. As proud members of this club, we were all guided by this great man's example of the Aloha Spirit, which he gave so unselfishly.

His motto of "Never say die!" taught us to never give up, to seek our dreams, and to always reach for the stars. That has since been my belief and I am very honored to present his great inspiration in my Hālau Hula o Na Kamaliʻi Nani o Lahaina (The Beautiful Children of Lahaina).

To teach is to touch a life—forever! Uncle Jimmie certainly touched my life with his teachings. And for all of you who touched my life along this journey and for all the keiki who have been a part of my life, all of you have added so very much aloha to my understanding of this great word!

Jan's hula hālau, Hālau Hula o Na Kamaliʻi Nani o Lahaina (The Beautiful Children of Lahaina) encourages children to learn the traditional dances of Hawaiʻi.

Practicing Aloha from Oklahoma to Punaluʻu

Ron Neal

I felt the Aloha Spirit very early on here in Hawaiʻi. I had been raised on a cattle ranch in rural Oklahoma and I knew (or was related to) many people in the community. You waved at everybody who passed by and they waved back. That was the same feeling I had from my arrival in Honolulu in 1969.

I had just finished classes at the University of Tulsa. A friend, who was stationed on Oʻahu during his two-year stint in the Marines, returned home to Oklahoma. He told such wonderful stories of Hawaiʻi that we caught a ride to the West Coast and for $80, flew into Honolulu.

People were friendly, but it was not until I moved out to Punaluʻu in the country, that I started to meet some of the local families who opened their hearts and doors to me. I worked in Waikīkī at Nick's Fishmarket and thumbed a ride home when I got off at 11 PM. I was home in forty-five minutes every night because of someone's aloha! I was invited to lūʻau celebrations and welcomed wherever I went. Trust and respect were given to you from the start, and it was up to you to keep it by your actions—or lose it the same way.

Now I am at home in the Islands. Both of my children were born in Hawaiʻi. I know they have picked up on these values. But it is much harder to give so freely nowadays.

I remember one trip to Haleakalā, my buddy had rented Hōlua Cabin and we were the only ones there. We were playing cards about midnight when there was a knock on the cabin door. I opened it to find a young man who had just arrived on Maui, hitched a ride up to the crater and hiked in. He was wearing rubber flip-flops and carrying a suitcase. It was freezing outside. My buddy wanted to turn him away but I said, "Let's give a little back of what we had been given so freely." I invited him into our cabin and he tended the fire for the rest of the night. It's the small things given that represent aloha.

Smile, open up, don't honk at others on the road, wait your turn, give somebody a ride home. Perpetuate the righteousness!

Ron is the president of Rimfire Imports, a food wholesale company on Maui.

A Tsunami is Coming,
A Tsunami is Coming

Louise Rockett

My mother was obsessed with end of the world scenarios. She passed before Y2K, but believe me: that was right up her alley, along with 2012. Weaned on the Depression and married on D-Day, she was quite imaginative, and some of her Chicken Little fears rubbed off on me.

Growing up, there were lots of dress rehearsals in our house; so, when the phone rang at 4 AM,, I felt I had been primed for the moment from the day I was born.

"Mom, you've got to leave your house. A tsunami is coming. A tsunami is coming," I heard a profoundly stressed voice announce. My eyes popped open. It sounded just like mom. Was she channeling through my daughter?

"Nicole?" I asked.

"Mom," she said with authority. "There was an earthquake in Chile. A tsunami is coming. You have to leave your house."

I had taken Hawaiian geology at UH-Hilo; this disaster script I knew by heart. I live in Kapoho on the Big Island, on a road at the edge of the world. It's literally falling into the ocean, a geological condition called a subsiding zone. According to a study, Kapoho is the single most dangerous place to live on the shoreline in the state of Hawai'i. If there was a tsunami or hurricane warning, there is no question about evacuation.

So why would a disaster-phobic freak live here? Well, it's like living in a Maxwell Parish painting. Below sea level, we have our own tidal pool, complete with fish that spill over onto the lawn at high tide. At night, the moon and stars seep through the canopy of palms. I often tell friends, "When the wave comes, I'm on a springboard to nirvana."

"Mom?" Nicole asked, this time more agitated.

"I'm up," I answered wide awake. "I have to call Carol," I said disconnecting. I wasn't worried about my daughter; she lived Upcountry on Maui. But Carol is my older sister and she was house-sitting down the street. No questions asked; I dialed her number. She knew the drill, and I was playing my part.

One ring, two rings, three, and then four. I was sweating. Did I dial the wrong number?

"Hello," a scratchy, sound asleep voice answered.

My thoughts were as abbreviated as my words.

"A tsunami is coming. A tsunami is coming. Get over here. Bring the truck," I blurted my lines and then hung up.

I jumped out of bed. An earthquake in Chile. This was no threat; it was real. I was running in circles. A tsunami is coming. A tsunami is coming.

Trained to turn on the radio, I channel surfed through the stations. Strangely, there was only music playing; no civil defense alerts. I keened my ears over the chorus of coqui outside; there were no sirens either. Wassup? I asked myself. I called the police.

"Aloha," the dispatcher's voice was so soothing; was I in a dream?

"This may sound strange, but my daughter just called. She told me a tsunami is coming."

She answered in a memorized, sing-songy kind of way, as if announcing flight information at the airport. "There was a magnitude 8.8 earthquake in Chile. A tsunami is headed our way, anticipated arrival 11 AM. The civil defense sirens will sound at 6 AM and every hour thereafter. No reason to panic. There is plenty of time."

"I live in Kapoho," I said.

"Oh," the sing-song went right out of her voice. "You'll have to evacuate." At that moment, my adrenalin kicked in.

I dialed Jake and Ellen, my dear friends who lived up the hill, and who had kennels, good grub, and plenty aloha in their hearts. Their son answered.

"A tsunami is coming. A tsunami is coming!" The words came faster each time. At that point, Jake joined the conversation, picking up the extension irritated at the unanticipated early morning wakeup call.

"Jake!" I jumped in before he could get mad. "A tsunami is coming." I was on fast forward, reciting the facts.

"First," his voice was steady, "calm down. We'll be there by six o'clock."

Thereafter, I was on auto-pilot, selecting which treasures to take and which to leave behind. Necessities were included in the packing, like computers, pet food, toothbrush, and my accounts receivable file.

In the meantime, Carol arrived, then Ellen and Jake. Talk was minimal, we were robots of few words. In the end, my sister and I consolidated our lives into one compact car and one truck, with Jake and Ellen stashing some odds and ends in their van.

Jake closed the house, turned off the gas and electric. It was getting light as we left the house. The neighborhood was justifiably astir.

"Has anyone checked on Beverly?" Carol asked Gina, our next-door neighbor.

"Check with Guy," Brandon threw in from his house across the street.

Our small community has a watch program that goes beyond a nighttime patrol and nīele (nosy) neighbors. Assured that everyone ninety years old or older was taken care of, Jake mapped out our evacuation plan. Then, caravan-fashion, we pulled out, pets and all; it was almost 7 AM. At the end of the street and at major intersections thereafter in the inundation zone, civil defense personnel were on duty. It felt safe.

I turned on the radio and on each channel there was a reassuring voice urging, "Act with Aloha." The message was chanted over and over and over again: act with aloha, act with aloha, act with aloha. It was like a mantra to ease our souls.

When I tuned in to 91.1, Hawai'i Public Radio, Howard Dicus was online. I was just passing Pāhoa. Howard's voice was as I had never heard it. His choice of music was eerily appropriate: John Adams's "Light over Water."

His recital of earthquake and tsunami facts sounded like a poetry reading of the most eloquent prose. "Light over Water" and Howard's vocals joined in symphony to celebrate the beginning of the day.

The sun was beginning to rise, and the golden globe filled my rearview mirror; while, at the same time, projecting a rainbow ahead in the early morning rainfall so common in Puna.

First, it was a mere pinkish-grey stretch, barely lifting off the ground. As the sun rose higher, the rainbow responded, and, with vibrant electric colors, the arc gradually filled in—first one rainbow and then another.

Light over water, indeed. The experience eclipsed all others that day spent watching the footage of the tsunami that came and went with no destruction

The all-clear was announced some eight hours later. The community was commended for keeping order. We were all blessed.

Aloha had saved the day.

Louise Rockett is an award-winning journalist and writer for Lahaina News. She still lives in Kapoho on the Big Island and in Nāpili on Maui, surrounded by love and aloha.

Comfort Me with Aloha

Nalani Aki

On Labor Day in 1987, as I lay basking in the sun on a beach called Yokohama in Honolulu, I had a thought of doing something spontaneous. So I went to the airport and caught the next plane to Maui! I wanted to stay only a day, but when I got to Maui fate took over.

I tried to rent a car but they were sold out due to the long weekend. I forgot about that part. I took a taxi to Lahaina, where I thought I could get a hotel room. After spending hours at a pay phone looking up hotel phone numbers, and having no luck at all, I decided to get a flight back to Honolulu. Well, of course, the planes were also sold out.

At this point I had no car, no hotel, and no extra clothes. I called home and asked, "Do we have any relatives on this island?" My sister said, as a matter of fact, yes we do. She gave me a phone number and I called my cousin.

We had never met before, but I needed help. I told her the story and she laughed. She came to my rescue all the way from Ha'ikū on the other side of the island to meet me at Pioneer Inn. After sweating and being on my own for hours, I learned the value of family ties! What comfort knowing that she had opened her arms to me with a hug of aloha.

Although aloha means the "breath of life," to me it means comfort.

Comfort is the Island way that if my child's friend has no place to eat or sleep, they are always welcome at my home.

Comfort is looking at the turmoil of today's economy, and hearing someone say, "It's okay, my friend. We'll get by."

Comfort is being accepted for who you are at present, not what you could have been.

Comfort is knowing that someone out there with open arms is just waiting to give you a hug of aloha.

We share many similarities, you and I. We are not so different after all. May you find comfort in the footsteps that you take through life.

Aloha aku, aloha mai: aloha given, aloha returned.

Nalani is the Hawai'i Department of Health Healthy Hawai'i Initiative Communities Program coordinator.

A Celebration—
and a Lesson on Living

Elizabeth Engstrom

Many years ago when I was young and living on O'ahu, I found myself between jobs and places to live at the same time. I decided to load a backpack with the bare essentials and head to the Big Island to spend some time vacationing and contemplating my future. I spent a month camping out in various campgrounds, hiking in pristine valleys and rainforests, meeting extraordinary people, and seeing astonishing things. The hospitality I experienced was amazing, and never once did I feel threatened or ill at ease.

There is one evening, however, that stands out in my memory and will forevermore.

Toward the end of my great adventure I had returned to Brown Beach Park in Kalapana, watching the sunset from my hammock strung up between two palm trees. I had journeyed to this black sand beach several times during my travels and on this particular summer evening there were several others camping in the park as well. I had some sort of food in my backpack and was just thinking about digging it out when a pickup truck came through the parking lot. A young man stood in the back of the truck yelling for everybody to come.

I was tempted, but tentative.

The truck stopped and two other young men got out of the truck and they fanned out into the park talking to the other campers. One of them approached me. They had had an extraordinarily good fishing day, he told me, and there was a birthday party and big celebration. Every camper in the park was invited.

He seemed nice. Local boy, clean cut. I looked around at the others, who were beginning to make motions as if they were going to join the party. I still needed to be convinced. Getting into strange vehicles with strange men was not my normal way of doing things, and yet there was something so appealing, so innocent and genuine about this invitation. As I saw the other campers look at each other and shrug, I finally agreed. I untied my hammock, threw it in my pack and jumped into the back of the pickup truck along with everybody else.

We couldn't have driven more than a couple of miles to an enormous house with a rocking party going on. The entire neighborhood must have been there. People swarmed over the house and spilled out over the grounds, talking, laughing, celebrating. The scent of grilled fish, along with the perfume of the flowers and the sea breezes gave the whole scene an air of unreality—something out of a movie. The owner of the house had already filled his ten children full of fish fresh off the grill and put them to bed, and now it was his turn to feed the entire neighborhood, as well as all the guests staying in the nearby campground.

At first I hung with the other campers, unsure of exactly why we were there, but as the evening wore on it became obvious. They were just sharing the wealth of their joy and good fortune. Though I was a stranger, and one of the few haoles there, everyone made me feel completely comfortable and at home.

The food was great, the music and dancing even better, and I was back in my hammock long before sunrise. And I had much to think about.

What couple—with ten children—feeds the neighborhood, including a dozen strangers?

People who live their aloha, that's who.

I left the Big Island a few days after that, flush with the good will of that family and their friends, and a whole new idea of aloha.

Visitors think aloha means hello or goodbye, but aloha is actually the breath of life. Invoking aloha is invoking that which connects us all, the recognition that we are one enormous family under the gentle guidance of the ultimate loving parent. Aloha is the blessing of our creator that we pass along to one another, with not only the word, but in myriad deeds of inclusion, generosity, faith, and kindness.

Many years have passed since that memorable night. Pele has completely changed the landscape of that part of the Big Island. Those ten children have grown and surely now have families of their own. So while much has happened, the aloha that couple showed me—one of a dozen strangers—that one night in celebration of abundance, has been passed down vertically through the generations of my children and grandchildren, and horizontally through life as I try to continue their example of selfless goodness and generosity to others.

Aloha is not just a word.

It is a way of life.

Liz is a teacher, minister, and author. Her book Lizard Wine *has been optioned for a film. She lives in Oregon.*

Aloha for the Newcomers

Gayle Selyem

When we were newcomers to the Big Island, it became known that we would be alone on Thanksgiving. Our neighbors literally came and got us—and brought us to their home to be with them and their family and friends!

We were embraced by the warm and welcoming spirit of those around us. It was very sweet, and from that day we were never alone on any holiday.

This seems to be something present on all the islands that we have visited. Those with the Spirit of Aloha in their hearts carry a quiet kind of peace, contentment, and happiness.

This story was submitted via the Practice Aloha website. www.PracticeAloha.org

Aloha—Welcome Home!

Elisa Southard

My husband Will and I have visited Maui seven times, each time anticipating the dance of the waves and the cloak of the banyan tree welcoming us and blessing our transition from the rush-a-day world of the mainland. We try to bring that calm feeling home with us.

Aloha to me is a smooth transition. A relaxed state of mind helps you through a major decision, such as switching jobs, getting married, or moving. In essence, you are better able to say hello to a new situation and bid a former one farewell.

Recently, Will's ninety-four-year-old father, Ed, realized it was time to move to a retirement home. The home he chose had multiple elevators, numerous entrances, and countless hallways. With failing eyesight, how smooth would this transition be?

A widower, Ed lived alone for almost eight years before moving into this new environment with over one hundred residents. "Remember, Ed, you were the president of the chamber of commerce. You'll know everyone in a few weeks," I mentioned as we negotiated the maze of halls.

I said a prayer that he would make friends quickly as he countered, "Well, I'm not as young as I was then. I can't see well."

An apartment had just opened up on the first floor, complete with a beautiful lanai, overlooking a lush lawn, surrounded by trees and benches, where he could inhale the morning. We noticed several hanging plants that belonged to his neighbor. "Well, looks like you'll get along with your neighbor, Ed. Another green thumb!"

Then Friday arrived, with the delivery of his new furniture at noon. My sister-in-law and I stood in the living room watching as the sofa was nudged into place. Ed walked out to his lanai, and soon we heard voices. "Ah, finally a face to go with the hanging plants," I thought as I heard Ed talking with his neighbor.

We walked out onto the lanai and aloha showered on all of us. I saw Ed talking to my own friend Marge! Then I remembered her mother had moved into this same retirement complex. Of course, we didn't know what apartment Robbie lived in. All concern about Ed's making friends dissolved as we exchanged hellos and hugs. I could see delight in Ed's eyes as a new almost-family friend offered the gift of a soothing transition: Aloha, welcome home.

Elisa is the owner of MarketSkills and the author of Break Through the Noise. She delivers motivational lectures for business owners and writers. She lives in Benicia, California with her husband, Will.

Aloha at Little Beach

Dario Campanile

I experienced a perfect example of Practicing Aloha five years ago at Little Beach on Maui. I was body surfing by myself when suddenly a wave crashed me on the hard floor of sand. It felt like I got hit by a truck. I badly dislocated my right shoulder and suffered a blow to my lower back.

I struggled to get out of the water and realized that the only way to avoid the excruciating pain was to hold my right arm straight in the air over my head. I felt lost and helpless. I was looking around dazed and confused when a man came up to me.

He managed to dress me up and carry all my belongings and helped me to climb back over the rocks to Mākena Beach all the way to the parking lot. Soon after that the fire department, ambulance, and police came to my rescue.

I have forgotten his name unfortunately, but I will never forget that act of compassion toward me from a stranger. I really felt the power as he Practiced Aloha that day.

Strangely enough, a few years later I was swimming at the same spot and suddenly I heard a call for help. A man had been pulled out to sea with the undertow. Without thinking I swam toward him and then realized he was a really big guy. There was no way I could save him. I yelled toward the shore for help and luckily another person came to assist me. It took both of us but we were able to save the man's life.

I guess being in Hawai'i, on the beach or anywhere else, Practicing Aloha and feeling the Aloha Spirit can become contagious.

Dario is an extraordinary fine artist. He exhibits his art at galleries in San Francisco, Laguna Beach, Aspen, Las Vegas, and Hawai'i.

Kamaʻāina and Malihini

Rhonda Faleafine

To Practice Aloha, share the spirit of Hawai'i's culture and way of life with each kama'āina (local) and malihini (newcomer) that comes your way.

Rhonda is the owner of A Royal Hawaiian Affair Wedding & Event Planners.

To Be Reminded

Julie Yoneyama

It was the day after Christmas. I was at the commuter airport waiting for my flight back to Kapalua when the airlines announced that my flight had been cancelled. I approached the courtesy counter when a woman tapped my shoulder and told me that my money was coming out of my pocket. Little did I know that small gesture would turn into one of the most touching encounters I ever had.

There were only a dozen people on that cancelled flight, and we were all instructed to run to the next terminal to catch the rescheduled Hawaiian Airlines flight. It was leaving in less than twenty minutes! Of course, I had to struggle with two carry-ons filled with omiyage, the local snacks and goodies you always brought back to friends and family—not only during the holidays but even if it was just an inter-island day trip! (Those were the days: two carry-on bags and wine that could go through security.)

When we landed in Kahului we waited for our luggage in baggage claim. But the last-minute transferees were left stranded, looking at each other. I recognized the lady who had told me about my money, and we gravitated toward each other. I introduced myself. My Good Samaritan said her name was Angela and that she was traveling with her husband, Matt. As we waited for the possibility of our bags arriving on the next flight, I busted out my cookies and snacks as we got to know each other.

Angela and Matt were from Virginia, and were only on Maui for a few days. "Matt prefers places where there's gambling," she said smiling. Another passenger, Kathy, owned a jewelry shop on Front Street that sold whale ivory. I found that such a coincidence because in my handbag was an elephant ivory bracelet that my grandmother passed on to me. I showed my new-found friends the antique ivory shaped into pīkake beads. Kathy said she had whale ivory earrings at her store that matched.

After three more flights arrived and still no bags, I decided to take charge, and six of us shared a Speedi Shuttle to the Westside. Hawaiian Air was going to deliver our bags later but unfortunately for Matt and Angela, they didn't pack extra clothes in their carry on.

The ride to Lahaina went quickly since we all enjoyed the company, conversation, and more of my goodies. I then invited Matt and Angela to the Old Lahaina Lūʻau where I worked. We all exchanged numbers and I told Kathy that maybe someday I'd be by to get those matching earrings. One by one we were dropped off. As everyone departed the shuttle, they were sent away with something from my goodie bags.

Two days later, Matt and Angela attended the Old Lahiana Lūʻau as my guests. After the lūʻau, they waited for me to get off work so I could give them a ride back to their hotel, but first we wanted to stop in and say aloha to Kathy at her store.

Once we got there, Matt and Angela picked out a couple things and Kathy showed me the earrings. They were a perfect match, but way over my budget. I knew I would have to wait quite awhile to get them.

As Kathy finished ringing up the purchases, she reached over the counter and handed me a piece of paper. I was a little confused. It was a certificate of authenticity—for the ivory pīkake earrings! At first I didn't understand, and then it hit me. I turned to Matt and Angela, who were grinning from ear to ear.

Angela gently took my hand and said, "Indulge us, Julie." I got teary-eyed. I was speechless and after it all sank in, Matt said, "You made our trip special, sharing your food and your hospitality." No one had ever done something like that for me—and they both said the same thing back.

That was the last time I saw them. I usually save those earrings for special occasions, but after writing this, I realize that I need to wear them more often to remind me that Practicing Aloha isn't limited to those of us who live in Hawai'i.

Julie is both a dancer and in management at the Old Lahaina Lū'au.

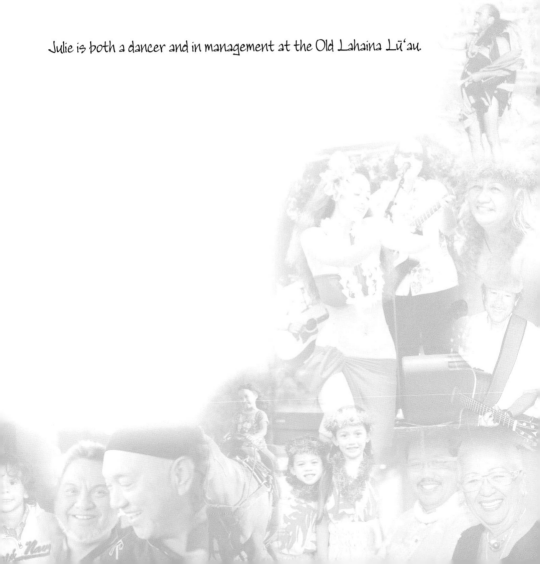

Aloha Lei

John Severson

When I arrived in the Islands in the fifties, lei sellers would park their old trucks in strategic spots—and leave them. Every day they would bring their beautiful flower work to display, and when pau, close the truck and amble home. It took a concerted lack of effort to let the truck virtually take root and the traffic cop smell the flowers, while the lei seller surrounded everyone with aloha.

John is the founder of Surfer Magazine and is a surf culture artist.

Aloha is Love

Pi'ilani Schneider

Born and raised in Hawai'i, we've been blessed to live with aloha. We are lucky we never had to "practice" it! We were raised with the spirit of loving each other unconditionally. My granny taught by example. Now we must pass this on, by example.

If you want to know aloha, please, give it yourself, but expect nothing in return. You give because you love and for no other reason.

Pi'ilani is an actress and photographer who lives on O'ahu.

Practice Aloha
In the Kitchen

Aloha makes life delicious! Sharing a rainbow-colored shave ice or slurping steaming noodles after a day at the beach … ahh, life is good.

A special kind of aloha can be found in the water, fruits, fish, taro, and all the other local foods in Island kitchens. Anyone can enjoy it by simply preparing a meal and gathering around the dinner table with friends.

The stories in this chapter were written by Hawai'i's favorite chefs. As a way to share the aloha, in the way they know best, almost every story is accompanied by a recipe that features the flavors of Hawai'i. Enjoy!

My Recipe for Aloha— and Beef Stew

Sam Choy

Practice Aloha is a simple recipe. Stir in a lot of caring, season with love, and sprinkle generously with happiness. But the most important ingredient is living pono (living pure) every day of your life.

Best Beef Stew
Serves 8

4 pounds chuck roast, cut up
Salt and pepper to taste
Enough flour to dust meat (about 1 cup)
2 cloves garlic, crushed
1 small onion, minced
½ cup celery leaves
5 cups beef stock or broth
2 cups chicken broth
1 ½ cups tomato paste
3 medium carrots, chunked
4 potatoes, chunked
2 medium onions, chunked
4 stalks celery, chunked
½ cup salad oil
Enough mochiko (rice flour) and water to thicken broth

Sprinkle beef with salt and pepper, then dust with flour. Heat salad oil in a Dutch oven or a large heavy pot. Brown meat with garlic, minced onion, and celery leaves about 10 minutes on medium or low-medium, until well browned. Keep stirring to avoid burning.

Drain oil. Add beef stock, chicken broth and tomato paste. Bring to a boil, then reduce to simmer. Cover and cook 1 hour, or until beef is tender.

Add carrots and potatoes; cook 5 minutes. Add onion chunks and celery and cook 10 minutes more. Adjust seasonings with salt and pepper.

If needed, thicken broth with a bit of mochiko/water mixture.

Sam Choy is one of the most recognizable chefs in Hawai'i. He is an award-winning restaurateur, and his best-selling cookbooks help home chefs cook with the flavors of Hawai'i.

Sharing the Mahi-Mahi

Beverly Gannon

The warmth of a meal prepared with love and passion.

Cooking all day with family and friends.

Cutting and chopping, stirring, and tasting, and then setting a large table with platters and bowls of food to be served family-style for everyone to choose what they want.

Passing food around the table, hands touching hands.

Bowls of pasta and platters of fish crisscrossing the table so that every morsel of food hits your plate.

Lovingly touching the person sitting next to you.

Warm food, warm bodies, warm laughter, full stomachs.

That's the Aloha Spirit!

Panko-Crusted Mahi-Mahi
(over a Garbanzo Bean, Portuguese Sausage and Manila Clam Stew)
Serves 6

    1 cup panko (Japanese-style bread crumbs)
    ¼ cup chopped fresh flat-leaf parsley
    2 teaspoons garlic salt
    6 (4-ounce) filets of mahi-mahi
    salt and pepper to taste
    ½ cup Dijon mustard
    3 tablespoons olive oil
    1/2 cup finely chopped onion
    1 teaspoon finely chopped garlic

1 cup thinly sliced spicy Portuguese sausage

2 cups garbanzo beans (canned), rinsed and drained

1 cup fish stock or clam juice

1 cup seeded coarsely chopped tomatoes

2 pounds Manila clams

2 tablespoons coarsely chopped cilantro

2 tablespoons canola oil

1 tablespoon fresh lemon juice

In a pie plate or similar dish, mix together the panko, parsley, and garlic salt. Salt and pepper the mahi-mahi fillets. Spread one side of the fillet with mustard. Press the fish, mustard side down, firmly into panko mixture to coat.

In a medium sauté pan, over medium high heat, pour in olive oil. Heat until hot, but not smoking. Add onions and cook 3 minutes or until they are softened. Add garlic and sausage. Cook for 3 minutes, stirring as needed. Add garbanzo beans and sauté 1 minute.

Add fish stock and cook 2 minutes. Add tomatoes and bring to a boil until liquid is reduced by half. Add clams on top of the liquid. Cover the pan to steam the clams. Cook until clams open, 3 to 4 minutes. Remove lid and any unopened clams. Stir to incorporate clams into the soup. Add chopped cilantro. Set aside and keep warm.

Add oil to a second medium sauté pan over medium high heat. Heat until very hot. Add mahi-mahi fillets, crust side down, and cook 2 minutes or until the panko crust is golden brown. Turn fillets over and turn heat down to low. Cook fish another 3 to 4 minutes until just cooked through.

Place a large ladle of garbanzo and sausage mixture in center of bowl. Top with a piece of mahi-mahi, drizzle a bit of the lemon juice over each bowl and enjoy immediately.

Bev is a busy woman! She is a cookbook author, restaurateur (most notably her Hali'imaile General Store), and caterer to the stars. She also created the Island-inspired menus for Hawaiian Airlines.

Only in Hawai'i: A Kālua Pig BLT

Alan Wong

Aloha is a part of Hawai'i. People around the world automatically think about Hawai'i when they hear the word "aloha," similar to how "pineapple," "Diamond Head," and "Waikīkī Beach" are all synonymous with Hawai'i.

Aloha can mean hello or goodbye. It can also mean caring, loving, and hospitality, as in, "Show 'em some aloha."

The word "aloha" carries an energy of its own. It embraces openly the concept of honoring, valuing, and welcoming others—the inclusion of everyone rather than exclusion—as if part of your 'ohana.

In the hospitality industry we use the term "Aloha Spirit" often. What makes Hawai'i unique are its people and culture. The Aloha Spirit, or, rather, the people who have the Aloha Spirit in them, is what makes people come back to Hawai'i time and again.

I get asked the question: "Is Hawai'i Regional Cuisine (HRC) re-locatable to another part of the world?" While some concepts are, others are not. Just as some ingredients are specific to Hawai'i, so too are the culture and the concepts of HRC.

Similarly, I feel the Aloha Spirit is unique to Hawai'i. To cook with aloha means happy guests, and that is what we do. We make people happy.

Kālua Pig BLT
Serves 1

    1 onion bun
    1 tablespoon butter, unsalted
    1 ½ tablespoon Boursin cheese, garlic flavor
    2 pieces bacon, cooked
    1 slice of grilled onions
    ½ cup kālua pig
    2 tablespoons Lomi Tomato (recipe follows)
    1 slice Hāmākua Springs tomato
    1 leaf Mānoa lettuce

    Cut the onion bun in half. Spread butter on each half and toast on a griddle. When the bun is grilled to your liking, spread the Boursin cheese on each half.
    Layer bacon, grilled onions, kālua pig (drained of liquid), lomi tomato, tomato slice, and Mānoa lettuce on the bottom half of the bun. Cover with the top half of the bun, and cut the sandwich in half. Serve immediately.

Lomi Tomato
Makes 1 ¾ cup

    1 cup vine-ripened tomato, diced
    ½ cup sweet Maui onion, finely diced
    ¼ cup scallions (green part only), finely sliced
    Salt, to taste
    Chili pepper water (optional)

    In a small bowl, combine the tomato, onion, and scallions. Season with salt. Add the water to achieve the desired texture. Refrigerate until needed in an airtight container. The lomi tomato will keep in the refrigerator for up to two days and the leftovers can be eaten on their own or as a side dish.

Alan is is the author of New Wave Luau and ten-time winner of the Hale 'Aina and 'Ilima awards for Restaurant of the Year and Best Restaurant. He is chef/owner of Alan Wong's Restaurant and The Pineapple Room in Honolulu, and also has Alan Wong's Hawai'i in Tokyo Disneyland.

Aloha for the Growers of Our Food

Peter Merriman

It was Christmas morning, 1989. I was at home in Puakō on the Big Island when the phone rang.

"Hi, my name is Richard Ha. I grow bananas in Kea'au," said the voice on the other end of the line. "You don't know me, but I know how much you do for the farmers in Hawai'i. I just wanted to say thank you."

That was our brief telephone introduction, but since that time I have gotten to know Richard as an amazing person and one of the great farmers of Hawai'i. He was the very first banana farmer to receive the ECO O.K. award by the Rainforest Alliance, which indicates he Practices Aloha for the land as well as for people.

I will always remember this inspiring man taking time on his Christmas morning to say mahalo to a stranger. That's Practicing Aloha!

P.S. I will continue to promote Hawai'i Regional Cuisine and raise awareness among residents and visitors alike, so we have a better understanding of good food—really good food—and how good food positively affects our families, our community, and our economy.

Merriman's Grilled 'Ahi with Coconut Curry
Serves 6 to 8

Curry
1 teaspoon Indian curry powder
2 tablespoons fresh grated ginger (Thai ginger if available)
2 stalks lemongrass, chopped fine
½ cup clam juice
1 cup coconut milk
4 kafir lime leaves (or 2 teaspoons lime rind poached in boiling water for 15 seconds)
2 teaspoons nam pla (fermented fish sauce; also called nuoc nam)

Fish
6 skinless 'ahi steaks, 1 to 2 inches thick, 6 to 7 ounces each
2 tablespoons vegetable or olive oil
salt and pepper

In a dry sauce pot, sauté curry powder over medium heat 1 minute until aroma fills the air. Add ginger, lemongrass, and clam juice. Simmer for 10 minutes. Stir in coconut milk; use as much of the thick cream as possible. Simmer for 5 minutes, then turn off heat. Crumble or fold lime leaf and add to sauce. Season with nam pla, salt, and pepper. Hold warm until ready to serve.

Make certain grill is very hot. Brush and season one side of 'ahi steaks.

Cook 'ahi on first side until the fish turns light in color ¼ of the way up the steak. Turn and cook for ½ the amount of the time as the first side.

Note: You do not need sashimi-grade 'ahi for this recipe. Select medium-grade. This dish goes well with sweet potatoes

Peter uses 90% local product in his menus, a standard unsurpassed within the Hawai'i culinary world. Many of his growers farm organically. A founding member of the Hawai'i Regional Cuisine (HRC) movement, he is the chef/owner of several top-rated restaurants on three Hawaiian Islands: Merriman's Waimea and Market Café in Kohala on the Big Island of Hawai'i; Hula Grill on Kāʻanapali Beach, Maui; and Merriman's Po'ipū, Kaua'i.

Mom's Aloha— and Asian Crusted New York Steak

D. K. Kodama

For me, "Aloha" has one simple definition: Mom.

My mother, Sandy Kodama, always was and always will be the embodiment of aloha. At all our restaurants we have a service standard that we call "Service with Aloha" or "How Mom (Kodama) would do it."

She would take care of guests like no one else did. She would babysit a customer's child so the parents could enjoy their meal like adults. She always had a smile on her face and would take the time to talk to every guest and become like the hostess of a party in her own home. She would drive people back to their hotels or sometimes even to the airport to make it more comfortable and easier for them—and to save them a taxicab fare!

She even took people she just met around the Island and showed them the sights. She really loved to talk to people, to get to know them and, as she put it "to make friends." During her life, she made many, many friends. At her funeral, thousands and thousands of her friends came to bid her aloha.

Throughout her life, she gave and gave of herself without ever giving a thought to what might be "in it for her." She simply loved to give and to make other people happy. That is aloha to me.

Asian Crusted New York Steak with Tomatoes in Vinaigrette
Serves 2

    2 (10-ounce) New York strip steaks
    1/4 cup salad oil (vegetable, canola, olive oil or mixture) divided
    1 tablespoon Asian Spice Mix (recipe follows)
    4 tablespoons sherry vinaigrette (recipe follows)
    1/2 cup tomatoes, grape or cherry, halved
    2 teaspoons chives, chopped into ¼-inch lengths

Asian Spice Mix
    ¼ cup shichimi togarashi (Japanese 7-spice blend)
    ¼ cup furikake (Japanese seasoning)
    ¼ cup black pepper, cracked
    1 tablespoon thyme, whole dried
    2 tablespoons granulated sugar
    1 tablespoon Hawaiian salt
Mix ingredients to make 1 cup of spice mix. Wrap and store.

Sherry Vinaigrette
    1/4 cup sherry vinegar
    2 ¼ teaspoons granulated sugar
    2 ¼ teaspoons Dijon mustard
    2 ¼ teaspoons Maui onion, peeled and finely minced
    3/4 cup olive oil

Blend the vinegar, sugar, Dijon, and onions in a mixing bowl. Slowly whisk in the olive oil by hand. This will make 1 cup of vinaigrette. Wrap and store in the refrigerator.

To Prepare Dish

Preheat oven to 400°F. Heat a large sauté pan over medium high heat.

Meanwhile, lightly baste steaks with about 1 tablespoon of salad oil. Crust both sides of the steaks with the Asian Spice Mix. Add enough of the remaining salad oil to lightly coat the sauté pan and add steaks. Pan-sear steaks golden brown on each side. Transfer into oven and cook to desired doneness.

Remove and allow steaks to rest for a minute. Slice steaks into ¼-inch thick slices. Transfer and plate on serving plates.

Combine and toss together the tomatoes, chives, and sherry vinaigrette. Garnish steak with the tomato-chive mix.

D. K. is a master restaurateur. The DK Restaurant Group includes the award-winning Sansei restaurants on Oahu and Maui, d.k. Steakhouse, and most recently two restaurants showcasing tapas on the menu!

Cooking (an Omelet) for a Friend

Ron Sambrano

Aloha is a great meal cooked by a friend. Even though they may have burnt the steak, it came from the heart, and that is aloha. We live, and laugh, and cry together, through good and bad. Aloha means to care, to be genuine, to be real.

Ron's Breakfast Open-Face Omelet
Serves 2

3 eggs, beaten (grade AA, preferably organic)
1 teaspoon cumin
Pinch of sea salt
2 tablespoons vegetable oil

Prepare the topping ingredients listed below; set aside.
Whisk eggs, cumin, and salt in a bowl.
Heat a nonstick pan over medium high heat. Add vegetable oil, fry up the eggs until golden brown on both sides (about 3 minutes per side).
Set the round cooked golden egg on a platter. Tent it with foil to keep warm.

For the topping
2 tablespoons vegetable oil for sautéing
1 teaspoon minced garlic
1 teaspoon minced shallots
6 to 8 ounces diced chicken breast

1 cup brandy for flambé
1 cup heavy cream
Pinch of thyme
Pinch of dill weed
1 teaspoon garlic powder

1/4 cup cooked sliced bell peppers
1/4 cup cooked sliced round sweet onions
1/4 cup cooked sliced mushrooms
Sea salt and pepper to taste
Grated Parmesan cheese and chopped parsley for garnish

In the same nonstick pan, heat the oil and add in the minced garlic and shallots until the aroma is present. Add in the chicken dices and cook through until brown.

Remove pan from heat source. Add in the brandy. Ignite the brandy with a match to flambé. Return to heat and cook off the alcohol for about a minute or two.

Add in the heavy cream and cook for about 2 to 3 minutes until the liquid reduces and thickens.

Season with thyme, dill weed, and garlic powder. Add in the bell peppers, onions, and mushrooms. Season with sea salt and pepper to taste. Pour filling over the cooked egg.

Garnish with grated Parmesan cheese and chopped parsley.

Serve with toast and hash browns.

Ron demonstrates various cooking techniques in a humorous way on his website, CookingClips.com.

Broke Da Mouth Aloha

Lloyd Yokoyama

My company, Broke da Mouth Cookie Company, opened its doors seven years ago. It was my lifelong dream to own and operate my own business. My parents owned a restaurant so I knew the hours would be long. I work thirteen to fourteen hours a day and try hard to find a balance between work and everything else. In this busy and hurried world that we live in, Practicing Aloha is many times easier said than done.

I work hard, but I love it because I make a product that people can enjoy so much. I've had people tell me that my Queen Emma cake is better than sex!

I have one story to share that touched my heart the deepest. While chatting with one of my customers, she told me she had cancer. She explained to me that she had always loved my Queen Emma cake, but now on days when she had her treatments, she was not able to hold anything down except for a slice of this wonderful cake. She then thanked me for being in business and for making her this cake that was making a difference in her life.

My customers share their aloha with me, and I try to pass it along to others. Whether it is wishing a customer a good day or spending a few minutes talking with customers to laugh and get to know them, we can practice sharing the gift of aloha every day.

Personally, I'd like to think that we put a little "sprinkle of aloha" in everything we bake.

Lloyd is the owner of Broke da Mouth Cookie Company.

Bread Pudding and Aloha

Mike deBruin

Aloha is the dessert of life. You probably could live without it, but who wants to?

This recipe is perfect for entertaining a large gathering of friends or an office of co-workers. It can even be an elegant contribution when you are assigned the dessert for a potluck! This rich and comforting bread pudding comes from Māla Wailea's own Sous Chef Mike deBruin.

Kā'anapali Coffee Bread Pudding

Half loaf sweet bread, Hawaiian or Portuguese (cubed)
1/2 cup brown sugar
1 quart heavy cream
1 cup ground Maui coffee (or a good quality coffee)
1 vanilla bean
7 whole eggs
1/4 cup dark rum
2 tsp. coconut extract
2 tsp. ground cinnamon
1 tsp. mace or nutmeg
a pinch salt
1/2 cup honey
3/4 cup maple syrup
1 cup creme fraiche (or sour cream)

1/2 cup caramel sauce
3/4 cup sweetened flake coconut
1/2 cup chopped dried fruit or nuts
Garnish: premium vanilla ice cream or whipped cream

Procedure

Preheat oven to 350°F. Toast sweetbread sprinkled with the brown sugar 10 minutes or until well toasted.

In heavy saucepot bring cream, ground coffee, and scraped vanilla bean to a boil. Remove from heat.

Whisk together eggs, rum, coconut extract, spices, salt, honey, and maple syrup.

Whisk creme fraiche (or sour cream) into the warm cream mixture, then strain into the egg mixture. Mix well.

Prepare ten 8 oz. ramekins or oven-safe bowls (coffee cups work well) with caramel sauce in the bottom. Put toasted bread and sugar into the cups; sprinkle coconut flakes and dried fruit or nuts on top of the bread. Carefully pour egg cream mixture (custard) over the bread until covered, press the bread down to make sure it is soaked with the custard

Bake in a hot water bath for 20 minutes in a convection oven or 25 to 30 minutes in a still oven. The bread should be golden brown and smelling absolutely fantastic.

Serve warm topped with your favorite ice cream or a dollop of whipped cream. (Makes 9-10 servings)

Mike is a baker and patisier (pastry chef) formally trained at the New England Culinary Institute in Vermont--the same school Alton Brown graduated from! Mike and wife Laura moved to Maui on a whim with a suitcase in each hand. While working as a cook at the Grand Wailea he responded to an ad that said "New restaurant opening in Wailea" and that was Māla Wailea where he is now the sous chef.

Aloha is Community

Jurg Munch

I grew up in Switzerland and my wife in Canada. When we came to Maui in 1997, I was surprised by the incredible generosity of the Lahaina community. Families opened their arms to welcome us and the true Aloha Spirit that was shared with us continues to amaze us today. Because of this, we decided to make this our home and raise our daughter in this gracious place. We feel lucky every day for all of the little things which make Maui special.

Firecracker Chicken
Serves 4

4 chicken breast pieces, boneless/skinless, cut into ¾-inch cubes
1 1/2 teaspoons cornstarch
1/2 egg white
1 1/2 teaspoons Shao Xing wine
1 tablespoon soy sauce
7 tablespoons vegetable oil, divided
1/2 cup raw peanuts
7 dried chili peppers
2 teaspoons minced ginger
1 small can water chestnuts, drained
2 teaspoons chopped scallions

Sauce
2 tablespoons mushroom soy sauce
1 1/2 teaspoons Shao Xing wine

1 tablespoons sugar
2 teaspoons balsamic vinegar
1 teaspoon cornstarch
1/4 teaspoon salt
1 1/2 teaspoons sesame oil

Mix the chicken cubes with cornstarch, egg white, Shao Xing wine and soy sauce in a bowl. Stir in one direction until well mixed. Don't over mix! Marinate for at least 30 minutes in the refrigerator or up to a couple of hours.

Heat one tablespoon of oil in a wok over medium heat. When the oil is hot, add the peanuts and fry until golden, stirring and tossing. As soon as they are golden, remove the peanuts from the oil. Drain them on a paper towel until cool.

Cut each chili pepper in half. Remove and discard the tips and seeds.

In a small bowl, mix together all the sauce ingredients.

Heat a wok over medium heat. When the wok is hot, add the remaining 6 tablespoons of oil. When the oil is hot, add the chicken and cook until it is 3/4 cooked, stirring and tossing gently.

Remove chicken from the oil with a slotted spoon and place in a colander or sieve to drain off the excess oil. Leave the oil in the wok and fry the red pepper pieces until they turn dark brown. Remove peppers with a slotted spoon and drain. Pour off remaining oil and reserve.

Increase heat to high. Add the ginger and stir-fry for 30 seconds. Add the chicken and toss. Add the peppers and water chestnuts and toss together. Add the sauce and stir until thickened. Turn off the heat and add the peanuts, mixing well.

Transfer to serving platter and garnish with scallions. Serve with steamed rice.

Jurg Munch is the chef/owner of the Lahaina Grill but at home, he really enjoys cooking Asian food. "After many years living in Hong Kong and cooking with my wife Linda, we love preparing her favorite family recipes."

Inspired Pineapple Ceviche

Chris Speere

Chris says his wife, Chef Becky Speere, is the inspiration for this wonderful ceviche.

Roasted Maui Gold Pineapple Thai Ceviche
Serves 8

2 cups Maui Gold pineapple, cut into 1/4-inch cubes
1 1/2 pounds fresh Island snapper (or 'ahi)
3/4 cup fresh-squeezed lime juice
1 cup julienned Maui onion, 1 1/2 -inch lengths
1 cup peeled, seeded, julienned cucumber
1/2 cup finely chopped fresh mint leaves
1/3 cup finely chopped fresh cilantro
1/2 cup finely chopped green onion
1/4 cup finely chopped fresh Thai basil leaves
3 tsp. Sriracha hot chilli sauce or 2 teaspoons minced Thai dragon
   pepper
1 cup coconut milk
2 tablespoons fish sauce
1 teaspoon Maui Brand Natural White Cane Sugar

Preheat oven to 350°F. Using a very sharp knife, cut off the crown of the pineapple. Cut the fruit in half and then into quarters. Trim off the center core. Cut the fruit from the shell and cut each spear into ¼-inch cubes.

Place the diced fruit onto a flat baking pan and roast in a 350-degree oven for 45 minutes or until the fruit turns golden brown.

Remove the pineapple from the oven and let it set at room temperature until cool.

Cut the fish into ¼ inch-cubes and place into a large glass bowl. Add fresh lime juice and marinate the fish in the refrigerator for 15 minutes. Do not drain.

To Serve

Remove the bowl from refrigerator and add the cooled roasted pineapple. Add the remaining ingredients: onion, cucumber, mint, cilantro, green onion, basil, hot sauce (or peppers), coconut milk, fish sauce, and sugar. Mix thoroughly.

Serve ice cold on crispy romaine lettuce leaves, with won ton pi chips or in chilled martini glasses.

Chris is the Maui Culinary Academy program coordinator. He and Becky are both well-respected contributors within the Maui culinary scene, and in addition to this recipe, their collaborative efforts include two daughters!

Sweet (Maui Onion Soup) Aloha
Shep Gordon

Shep Gordon's Maui Onion and Ginger Soup
Serves 14 to 16

8 tablespoons (1 stick) unsalted butter
12 Maui onions, peeled and thickly sliced
1 (4-inch) piece fresh ginger, peeled and grated
10 cups chicken stock
1 bottle of dry white wine (750 milliliters)
9 sprigs fresh thyme (or 1 tablespoon dried thyme)
2 cups half and half
Salt and freshly ground pepper

In a large stock pot or soup kettle, melt the butter over moderately high heat. Add the onions and ginger.

Reduce the heat to moderately low and cook until the onions are transparent, stirring often (about 15 minutes). Do not allow the onions to brown, or the soup will be bitter.

Add the chicken stock, wine, and thyme. Increase the heat to moderately high and bring to a boil. Reduce the heat to moderate and cook, slightly covered, for about 3 hours.

Working in several batches, puree the soup in a food processor or a food mill. Return the puree to the pot and add the half and half.

Bring to a boil over moderate heat.

Season with salt and pepper to taste.

Ladle into warm bowls and serve at once.

Shep is a gourmand who delights in cooking for his famous houseguests. He has even cooked dinner for the Dalai Lama!

Twin Tiki Necklaces

Ben Klein

It was a typical day at work. I was running around like crazy trying to do too many things at once. My kitchen support team simply stared in awe as I ran around in circles like a chicken that had recently been beheaded. Deliveries were late, the prep list was growing—so too was my frustration. In an effort to stem the tide of anger and frustration welling inside of me, I stepped out for one of my now notorious thirty-second smoke breaks.

As I paced around the break area plotting my next course of action, my eyes wandered across a disposable underwater camera that had been left under a tree. I really didn't think twice about it; I simply grabbed the camera, brought it inside, and re-embarked on my headless chicken journey.

An hour later I had forgotten about the camera, as the tide of frustration was reaching tsunami level inside of me. That's when I saw a pale-faced stranger peeking in through the back door.

"Can I help you?" I tried to say as politely as possible given the situation. The stranger asked if anyone had found a disposable underwater camera. I quickly grabbed it and gave it to him. He thanked me and went on his way with a smile. This alone had started to stem the tide of frustration and I was already feeling a little better about our situation at the restaurant. I figured, hey, at least we put a smile on someone's face today.

I returned to my work when to my surprise the stranger reappeared at the back door. I opened the door to see what was up now and he handed me two tiki god necklaces. He said they were small tokens of appreciation for rescuing the camera. The stranger went on his way with a smile, an infectious smile, which had begun to infect me.

I turned to my prep cook Teddy and saw a similar smile. He was also the father of twin seven-year-old daughters. Without a second thought—again, I probably didn't have time—I handed Teddy the necklaces. By now the infectious smile had become a "feel-good plague" as it passed through the kitchen. Teddy thanked me and dove back into his work with a renewed sense of vigor.

Needless to say the rest of the day was smooth sailing. I thought to myself about how such small acts of kindness had turned everyone's day around. We were part of a chain reaction of kindness and infectious happiness from me to the stranger, to Teddy, to the rest of the kitchen, to Teddy's daughters.

Suddenly I realized how simple, everyday actions can put forth a "community first and self second" attitude. That is what Practicing Aloha is all about and why it's so important in our lives.

Stir-Fried Brussels Sprouts
Serves 2

1 pound fresh Brussels sprouts
1 teaspoon sambal chili paste
1 teaspoon fish sauce
1/2 teaspoon sugar (preferably raw cane)
1 teaspoon sesame oil
1 tablespoon rice wine vinegar
1 tablespoon mirin (sweet Japanese rice wine)
1 tablespoon soy sauce
1 tablespoon water
2 tablespoons olive oil

Garnish

A pinch of sesame seeds

2 won ton wrappers (Cut in half, then into strips. Fry until crispy golden)

A few leaves of fresh mint, julienned

Remove bottom stems and quarter the Brussels sprouts.

Bring 4 to 6 quarts of well-salted water to a boil in a large pot. Place a large strainer so it is submerged in a large bowl of ice water. Boil the Brussels sprouts for about 2 minutes or until very al dente (firm to the touch).

Drain sprouts, then immediately place them in the ice water strainer. Drain again once they are well cooled. Allow the sprouts to dry in the strainer with a towel over top for 30 minutes or so.

Combine the remaining ingredients for the sauce (but not the oil and garnish ingredients). Stir well. Allow sauce to sit while Brussels sprouts dry.

Heat a large skillet with the olive oil over medium high heat until the oil is nearly smoking; add the well-drained sprouts until it is one thin layer in the pan. Be careful: they will splatter.

Cook about 1 minute. Do not shake or toss the pan. Check by turning one sprout with tongs to see if it is golden brown. (You may have to cook two batches depending on the size of your pan.) Toss gently and cook for another 30 seconds to 1 minute until just tender.

Remove to a bowl, let rest for 30 seconds and add half of the sauce. Toss well. Transfer to serving plate and garnish with sesame seeds, fried won ton, and mint just before serving.

Serve remaining sauce on the side for dipping.

Ben is executive chef of Māla Ocean Tavern in Lahaina, Maui. Not only a great chef, he is a true practitioner of Aloha.

Potato Chip Cookies

Vera Abercrombie

Sometimes all it takes is the memory of a special cookie to bring back the good memories and aloha of childhood. Neil Abercrombie shares this unusual recipe from his mom's recipe box. Enjoy!

Potato Chip Cookies
Makes 1 dozen cookies

½ pound margarine (2 sticks)
½ cup sugar
Dash of vanilla extract
1 ¾ cup flour
1 ¼ cups crushed potato chips
Confectioner's sugar (optional)

In large mixing bowl, cream butter and sugar. Add vanilla, then flour, and finally crushed potato chips. Mix well and chill for 30 minutes for ease in handling. Roll into 2-inch balls and press down with a fork on a greased cookie sheet.

Bake in 350-degree oven for about 15 minutes or until edges are brown. Sprinkle with confectioner's sugar.

Vera Abercrombie's cookie recipe, because of all that margarine and the potato chips, bakes up a cookie that is similar to a churro, pizzelle, or fried cookie. They are super easy to make and positively addictive!

Aloha in the Caramel Miranda

Mark Ellman

Can food induce the Aloha Spirit? Well, this dessert proves that it certainly can help. This is Chef Mark's signature dessert and it is an explosion of taste and color.

Mark likes to include a "novelty" food item in his dishes to get folks talking. Here it's the baby coconuts, or coquitos. Look for these tiny coconuts, no bigger than large marbles, in the produce specialty section. They can be eaten whole.

Serve Caramel Miranda on a big platter and let guests spoon their portions into individual bowls. Better yet, have everyone "go for it" straight from the serving platter with long-handled iced tea spoons!

Caramel Miranda
Serves 4 generously

Caramel Sauce
2 cups sugar
½ cups water
¼ teaspoon cream of tartar
1 cup heavy cream
¼ pound unsalted butter

Suggested Fruits to include on the platter

1 cup diced fresh Hawaiian pineapple
1 cup diced fresh mango
1 cup diced strawberry papaya
1 cup baby coconuts (coquitos) or shaved coconut
1 cup fresh raspberries
1 cup fresh blackberries
1 cup banana, sliced on diagonal
½ cup dark chocolate chips or pistols, Hawaiian if possible
½ cup white chocolate, Hawaiian if possible
4 cups macadamia nut ice cream
fresh mint sprigs for garnish
½ cup diced macadamia nuts, roasted and unsalted

Method

In heavy sauté pan, whisk together the sugar, water, and cream of tartar over high heat. Stir constantly until it is golden brown. Remove from heat and whisk in the cream. Whisk in the butter. Keep the caramel sauce warm, but not hot.

Drizzle the caramel sauce on a large oven-proof plate or platter. Arrange the prepared fruit and chocolate on top. Carefully put plate in a pre-heated 350-degree oven. Heat until the chocolate is just melting.

Scoop the ice cream right on the middle of a very large plate or platter immediately before serving. Garnish the plate with fresh mint and sprinkle roasted diced macadamia nuts over it all.

Serve immediately with a great Hawaiian coffee and raw sugar.

Mark has been serving this dessert since his first restaurant on Maui, Avalon in the 1980s, but it never gets old. People love it and it is still featured on the menu at his Māla restaurants.

Stand Up for the ʻĀina

James McDonald

I remember coming to Hawaiʻi in 1980 as a teenager and saying to myself, "Wow!" The moment I stepped off the plane I knew this was the place where I wanted to live for the rest of my life. It really wasn't a difficult decision. I grew up in Philadelphia. Snow, rain, potholes versus sun, sand, and bikinis: it was a no-brainer.

I was living on Oʻahu and hanging out one typically beautiful day down at Fort DeRussy beach when I saw a girl throw a small piece of trash down. I don't remember if it was a cigarette butt or chewing gum wrapper, but I said, "What are you doing? Please don't do that! This is such a beautiful place and here you are throwing trash down?"

I really deplore people that litter. I just don't know what the mindset is. We are all living on this beautiful planet and to destroy that is weird to me. But anyway, after I had said that, a Hawaiian guy standing next to me whom I didn't even know looked at me and said "Eh, mahalo, brah."

He then said something in Hawaiian dialect and I thought to myself, "Cool." I could see in his eyes a genuine respect for what I had just done.

I wasn't looking for acknowledgement, but to have made a difference at that moment felt really good. My personal sense of Practicing Aloha despite my being a haole in a kanaka Hawaiʻi setting just made me feel that anyone can actually make a difference at any given time.

To this day I still have an avid belief in caring for the ʻāina that we have been so fortunate to inhabit. I hope anyone that reads this will do their part to take a moment and pick up that piece of ʻōpala or to have the courage to correct someone they see disrespecting the land.

James McDonald's Upcountry Ravioli Braised ʻUlupalakua Lamb with Maui Onion, Surfing Goat Cheese, and Oʻo Farm Cilantro Pesto.
Serves 8

Ravioli Filling
3 to 4 pounds ʻUlupalakua lamb shoulder
3 ounces canola oil
Salt and pepper
½ cup flour
8 ounces red wine
2 cups chicken stock
½ cup carrots, chopped
½ cup celery, chopped
½ cup leeks, chopped
3 tablespoons shallots, chopped
3 cloves garlic
2 bay leaves
3 sprigs, thyme
1 sprig rosemary
1 teaspoon coriander seed
1 teaspoon black peppercorn
4 juniper berries, crushed

Preheat oven to 325°F. Place a heavy pot over medium high heat. Add oil. Season lamb with salt and pepper, coat in flour, and brown on all sides. Drain oil. Add remaining ingredients from list above. Place lid or foil over pot. Put into oven for 2 1/2 hours or until fork tender. Remove from oven; remove meat from pot and strain. Reserve braising liquid (the ravioli will be simmered in this broth). Shred meat with two forks and cool.

4 tablespoons butter
2 cups Maui onion, diced
1 cup rutabaga, diced
½ cup flat parsley, chopped
Kosher salt and ground pepper, to season

Sauté Maui onion and rutabaga in butter until soft; season with salt and pepper. Cool and add to lamb along with parsley.

Pasta Dough
2 cups flour
2 cups semolina flour
½ teaspoon sea salt
6 large organic eggs
2 tablespoons olive oil (Arbequina)

Sift dry ingredients together and form a mountain. Make a well in the center. Crack eggs into the well and add oil. Whisk eggs gently with a fork, incorporating flour from the sides of the well. When mixture becomes thick, begin kneading with your hands. Knead for 10 minutes until dough is smooth. Dust dough and work surface with flour as needed. Wrap dough in plastic. Allow to rest at room temperature for 30 minutes. Roll dough out with a rolling pin or pasta machine to desired thickness.

Cilantro Pesto
2 cups cilantro
2 cloves garlic
¼ cup pine nuts
¼ cup Parmesan cheese, grated
2 cups olive oil (Arbequina)

Place pesto ingredients into a blender or food processor and purée into a paste.

Finish and Garnish
1 egg, beaten with 2 ounces water
1 biscuit Surfing Goat Dairy cheese
Fresh thyme sprigs for garnish

Brush dough with egg wash. Make ravioli by evenly spacing mounds of filling on ½ of the sheet of dough. Cover with remaining sheet of dough. Using a pizza cutter or sharp knife, cut out ravioli making sure the edges of the dough are crimped together to hold the filling. Simmer ravioli in lamb braising liquid until dough is cooked, about 8 to 10 minutes. Place on a plate. Garnish with goat cheese crumbles, thyme sprigs, and cilantro pesto.

Chef James McDonald has built a culinary empire on Maui with his restaurants I'O, Pacific'O, and The Feast at Lele. As an outgrowth of his commitment to use fresh locally grown products, he established O'o Farm and recently opened the 'Ʉina Gourmet Market.

Aloha is a State of Mind

Shirley Fong-Torres

The first afternoon that my daughter Tina and I set foot in Hawai'i in the summer of 1980, we both knew we would be returning time and again. Pleasure and business now put me on the jet back to the many islands of Hawai'i, or rather the many islands of Aloha.

Aloha is a state of mind. It is a wondrous sense of well being. When I am among my old and new friends in Hawai'i, I feel a spiritual connection. My smile is broader; my heart beats prouder. I am always happy in Hawai'i. I feel healthier; I feel prettier; I feel like doing more to bring laughter to those around me. I love the sunsets, the sunrises, the music! I applaud the chefs, the home cooks, the farmers, the food purveyors. I love the many cultural attractions, but most of all, I love the people of Hawai'i.

These days, I am privileged to do inflight videos to promote the various islands of Hawai'i. I am invited to judge cooking contests, teach Chinese cooking, participate in food and travel writers' conferences, and to set up Wok Wiz-Hawai'i special programs. It is always a joy to write about those experiences.

While I Practice Aloha in San Francisco, I can't wait to return to hug my many friends in Hawai'i.   Mahalo!

Shirley's Hand-Hacked Seafood Potstickers
Yield: approx 30 pieces

1/3 pound lean ground pork
1/3 pound minced baby shrimp and/or bay scallops
1 cup of napa cabbage
1 cup fresh spinach leaves
1 scallion, minced
3 cloves garlic
1 teaspoon fresh ginger
1 tablespoon soy sauce
1/2 teaspoon of 100% sesame oil
Pinch of white pepper

HAVE ON HAND one pound of potsticker* wrappers (about 30), small bowl of cold water, 12-inch nonstick pan with cover, 2 cups of chicken broth

To make filling, chop pork, seafood, cabbage, spinach, scallion, garlic, and ginger. Place mixture into a bowl. Add soy sauce, sesame oil, and white pepper.

To assemble potstickers, spoon 1 tablespoon of the filling into the center of each potsticker wrapper. Fold dough over to make a half-circle; moisten bottom half-circle with a small amount of water. Pleat edges firmly, forming 3 to 4 pleats on the top half-circle. Set each potsticker upright on a platter, so a flat base is formed.

Heat a 12-inch nonstick fry pan with 1 tablespoon oil. Place the potstickers close to one another. Brown the potstickers about 30 seconds. Pour in enough chicken broth to cover potstickers halfway. Cover and cook over moderate heat for 5 minutes until liquid evaporates. Use a spatula to remove potstickers carefully. Turn each potsticker over, dark side up, and place on a platter to serve.

*I prefer purchasing "suey gow" wrappers if they are available, as they are lighter, and you can taste more of the filling. I also prefer a nonstick fry pan over a cast iron pan because the nonstick fry pan requires less oil, and the potstickers slip out of the fry pan easily.

Have in little dishes an assortment of hot chili oil, vinegar, soy sauce, and sesame oil. Mix dip ingredients to suit individual taste.

Shirley Fong-Torres is the owner of WOK WIZ Chinatown Tours & Cooking Co. based in San Francisco. She has written many books including In The Chinese Kitchen, Wok Wiz Chinese Cookbook, and The Woman Who Ate Chinatown. She can be seen on the Food Network, on the History and Discovery channels, and in the air on inflight videos for Hawaiian Airlines, Qantas Airlines, and JetBlue.

Aloha Tea for Healing

Eric Leterc

When someone I know gets a cold or flu, I prepare this special infusion. When I make this recipe, I use my positive feelings and love to heal the person. So, I am going to give you my secret potion. Try it next time someone is not feeling well.

3 to 4 branches of rosemary
A handful of thyme
A nice piece of ginger, smashed
4 to 5 cloves of garlic
1 lemon, sliced
3 cups of honey
5 star anise

Use a large pitcher (or use any container able to hold the heat). Place all of the ingredients inside the pitcher.

Pour some boiling water on the top of all the ingredients and stir. You must let it infuse for at least 15 minutes before you can start to drink.

Remember to add your positive feelings and love so that this Aloha Tea will give good energy to your friend.

Always cook and live life with aloha.

Eric was born and raised in France, but he has been a part of the culinary scene in Hawai'i since 1990. He is the Pacific Club's executive chef and even prepared the wedding feast for Bill Gates.

Practice Aloha
With Music

Aloha makes life harmonious on many levels. Could that be why music is one of the best ways to feel—and share—the Aloha Spirit?

The entertainers and musicians in this chapter spread aloha to the world through their music. It is their mission and their passion to make music that expresses the essence of the Islands. Their songs can fill us with joy or bring a tear to the eye.

When they play for us, we feel connected to one another.

Some Call it Aloha

Roland and Robert Cazimero

What does "Practice Aloha" mean to the Brothers Cazimero? Read Roland's lyrics to the song "Some Call It Aloha":

Some call it Aloha, We call it Love
Some say it's a yearning to have someone …

In this world that we Hawaiians inhabit at this time, it's often difficult to Practice Aloha. When our Islands have a population that is 51percent malihini (Hawaiian for a newcomer or guest), we need to work together in order to keep the idea of the Aloha Spirit alive.

Some call it Aloha, We call it Love …

In our travels as the Brothers Caz, we have found pockets of aloha world-wide. Knowing that, imagine how wonderful it would be to string these pockets into a global lei of aloha!

The song "Some Call It Aloha" featured in the story above, helped earn the Brothers Cazimero a nomination for the first Grammy award in the Best Hawaiian Music Album category. Their "chicken skin" performances honor the musicians and elders who paved the way for them, and include the chants, dances, and songs of their ancestors.

Mālama Ko Aloha

Keola Beamer

My inherent understanding of the word "Aloha" came as a beautiful gift from my Hawaiian 'ohana.

When we were very young, my mother, Nona Beamer, taught us the phrase, "mālama kō aloha." This meant that as human beings, we were to "cherish our love." We learned to love Hawai'i. We learned to love our planet. We learned to love one another.

As love informed reality, my life became enriched. I began to navigate the journey of my existence with decisions based on love, rather than fear. It was by giving aloha, that I received it, in more ways than I could ever express.

In my view, aloha is not just a thought. It is the path. It is the philosophical music of existence. And for its sweet, harmonic presence in my life, I am forever grateful.

Keola is a singer-songwriter, arranger, composer, and master of the Hawaiian slack key guitar. He wrote the classic song "Honolulu City Lights," which is still one of the all-time best-selling recordings in the history of Hawaiian music!

Light of the World ...
Aloha is the Answer

Michele and Todd Rundgren

When we were mainlanders, "Aloha" simply meant hello and goodbye.

When we vacationed regularly on Kaua'i, that changed. We started to feel aloha with the stories Mrs. Guslander told each night at the Coco Palms Hotel. While walking through the palm groves and Kaua'i's gardens, feeling the sand between our toes, we were greeted by calm smiles from the locals.

It wasn't until we moved to Kaua'i that we understood aloha. It isn't just a feeling; it is a state of being. It's being in a place where the scent of a flower many feet away can distract you. It's when you take time to watch a bird overhead or an ocean dance up and down the sand. It's when you are calm enough to hear the rain coming a whole minute before feeling its warm showers happily drench you. When you reach this state of aloha there is no need to rush through life, to honk your horn, or be easily angered.

We have learned that aloha is not only something to be felt but a feeling to pass on, to show, to give. It is so easily spread. Aloha is to give your patience, your time, your eyes, and your smile to others. Aloha is viral. If shown, it easily grows.

"Light of the world shine on me. Love is the answer.
Shine on us all, set us free, Aloha is the answer."

Michele and Todd Rundgren are both over-the-top performers. Michele performed with the rock group The Tubes and on Broadway. Todd has written, performed and produced many classic songs including "Bang on the Drum All Day" (the Carnival Cruise line theme), "Love is the Answer," and "Hello, It's Me." Or would that be "Aloha, It's Me" when they are at home on Kaua'i?

Easy Aloha

Tom Moffatt

Practice Aloha with something very easy to give: a smile.

Tom is the "Showman of the Pacific" concert promoter who brought the Rolling Stones and Elvis to Hawai'i.

Mom and Dad

Henry Kapono

Aloha is everything amazing. My mom lived it. She was the best cook in the world, and she always had something cooking on the stove whenever I'd come home from football practice. Of course, I wouldn't be alone. My friends were big guys and they ate a lot. My mom always had enough for everybody and she would feed us before she ate. If we ate it all, she just whipped something else up for herself and my five sisters and two brothers. Aloha: she lived it 24-7.

My dad was the Ambassador of Aloha. He did everything and anything for anybody and everybody—and he never made a fuss. I don't remember him ever saying "No."

I do remember when we would kālua pigs (five to ten pigs three hundred to six hundred pounds each) for the church. It was fun with everybody working the imu (ground stove). After the lū'au everyone else disappeared. But he, my brother, and I were the three-man clean up committee. My dad always made it fun to clean up no matter what it took and he always had a smile on his face. Aloha: he lived it 24-7.

You can't help but inherit this wonderful trait of Practicing Aloha that we in Hawai'i are so fortunate to have. My mom and dad passed it on to me. I live it, love it, and breathe it. It's part of my life and it's part of my music.

I always felt that Hawai'i is the heart of this planet. We live in the middle of the sea, thousands of miles away from the shores of other lands, yet we survive with an unconditional love and pride for each other and for our sense of place.

We have our problems like everyone else, but we overcome them and get the most out of our lives as we Practice Aloha.

Henry Kapono, one of Hawai'i's favorite singer-songwriters, has taken home numerous Nā Hōkū Hanohano awards (Hawai'i's Grammys) for Male Vocalist of the Year, Song of the Year, Single of the Year, and Album of the Year. He is also the author of the award-winning children's book, *A Beautiful Hawaiian Day*, has appeared in the films *Damien* and *Waterworld*, and has made many television appearances.

Shock Rock Aloha

Alice Cooper

Alice Cooper and Shep Gordon are long time friends and neighbors on Maui.

Being the king of shock rock and the scourge of rock and roll, one may not think there is much aloha in me. But my wife Sheryl and I have spent thirty-five years in and out of Maui. There must be aloha in me because it keeps showing up in my personality. But, mind you, never ever on stage!

Alice is the iconic hard rocker who literally invented the concept of the rock concert as theater. From his first hit, "Welcome to My Nightmare," his remarkable career includes platinum albums, sold-out tours, and career achievement awards.

Aloha is Shared with an 'Ukulele on YouTube

Jake Shimabukuro

Aloha is music, and music is good medicine. It brings people together, heals your soul, and inspires the world.

Jake is Hawai'i's virtuoso 'ukulele player, who broadened his fan base following a YouTube video. He is now spreading aloha in concerts around the globe. He has even played with Bette Midler for the Queen of England!

My Take on Practicing Aloha

Uncle George Kahumoku

My tūtū Emily Lihue Hoopale Dulay taught me that it's not what you say that is important, but what you do. Aloha is an action verb that places everyone else ahead of you. Aloha is not about me, it's about us—and our relationship toward each other.

One thing about our tūtū is that they "aloha," or love you unconditionally, no matter what you did wrong. But I am the judge and jury of myself and believe me: I'm not Mr. Aloha all the time.

Anyway, I tell you this just so you know I am for real. For some reason when I get behind the wheel, driving the winding road to and from where I live and farm in Kahakuloa, all the aloha I've got goes out the window. I turn into the New York cab driver from hell. I impatiently wish the tourists would just pull on the side and let us locals get on with our lives so we can get where we need to be. I can live without slow-driving tourists looking at the beauty of our islands or, worse yet, tourists stopped in the middle of the road to take photos of whales! For Christ's sake, pull on the side!

But I do Practice Aloha in my life. My grandmother was a healer who taught me that the huna, the secret of her healing, lay in her ability to visualize the sick person as being healthy. For instance, if he was a sick fisherman, she saw him as a fully recovered fisherman harvesting the blessings of fish from our great ocean. Same thing when she planted banana. She would drag the banana into the puka we had dug, making grunting sounds of the huge bananas we would be harvesting.

I learned this huna permeates our behavior when dealing with Aloha or Love. Love can overcome any hardship or challenge in life if we visualize it and bathe in the light of it. Some do it through prayer and meditation. However sometimes we have a hard time seeing what we want.

So for me I draw, write, and even cut out pictures of things that I want to achieve or create. I put them in my journal (or on the refrigerator) to remind me. Then I bathe myself in the light of Aloha. I leave it up to the Universe to connect me with those who can help me. I let it all go, so that it can come back to me again.

Sometimes I do get stressed out like everyone else. The trick that always works for me is to list all the blessings I have to be thankful for, and then I get myself back on track. Sometimes things don't turn out exactly how you thought they would. But most times, with aloha, life turns out better than you envisioned!

Because I want to do it all, I also trust in the power of aloha and surround myself with skilled people who can help me achieve my vision. We help each other … and kōkua through aloha breeds more aloha!

Anyway that's my take on aloha. From getting a parking space to living in your dream house, if it's done with aloha, it's yours.

George is a multiple Grammy and Hōkū award-winning master slack-key guitarist, songwriter, world-traveling performer, high school and college teacher, artist and sculptor, storyteller and writer, farmer and entrepreneur. He is about as Hawaiian as you can get, which is a nice thing to say about someone.

One Portagee's Aloha

Frank DeLima

Aloha is a word with a feeling of kindness, understanding, joy, comfort, peace, goodness, patience, and love all "rapped" up in a smile.

Frank is a comedian known for being able to turn just about any subject into a rap song. (Check him out on YouTube.) He keeps Hawai'i laughing as he deftly pokes fun at cultural stereotyping in his routines.

Aloha is Sharing

Carole Kai

My mother was a young girl in the 1920s with eight siblings. They were living in the Kahaluʻu Valley on Oʻahu among the Hawaiian families there who planted taro.

My grandfather and grandmother were hardworking people. They had to be, because they had nine children to feed! For weeks at a time, my grandparents had to work in Wahiawā, on the other side of Oʻahu. My grandfather was building the rock wall at Wheeler Army Base (it's still there) and my grandmother was a washerwoman for the railroad workers in Wahiawā.

The beautiful Hawaiian families in Kahaluʻu Valley knew that the Iwamoto children were by themselves for weeks at a time. It was very difficult for their parents to get back to Kahaluʻu daily because of lack of transportation. So, during dinnertime, the Hawaiian families would call the Iwamoto children.

"Ooo ee—E komo mai!" they would say.

The children in my mother's family joined the neighbor families, everyone sitting outside on a big lau hala mat. On the ground there would be a huge wooden bowl filled with fresh poi. On a large leaf (probably a ti leaf) placed in front of each person, there was a piece of fish, a piece of taro, a sweet potato, and whatever else they had to share. Everyone would use two fingers to eat poi out of the big bowl—and they ate to their hearts' content!

My mom loved Hawaiian food because of those days in Kahaluʻu Valley. She also adored the Hawaiians because they were loving, generous, kind, and happy. They were the true practitioners of aloha!

The Hawaiians believed in helping everyone because their belief was that any stranger could be a god. Hospitality was the Hawaiian way. That was the Aloha Spirit!

My mother grew up wanting to help people, the way she was helped. This was not to be because she became a single parent who had to work sixty hours a week just to keep her three children in clothes and food. This was a point of sadness for her, but I did not realize this until I became an adult.

It became my mission to do charitable endeavors in honor of my mother and God. God blessed my mother with good thoughts and intentions; they were passed on to me. That is why I started the Carole Kai Bed Race in 1974.

Over the years I've met many people who have inspired me, and I know my life is happier when I'm in service to support others. Practicing Aloha has made my life more enriched and blessed.

Carole Kai Onouye is the driving force behind two iconic Oʻahu charity events: the Carole Kai International Bed Race (1974 to 1994) and the Great Aloha Run (since 1985). Carole is also the producer of Hawaiʻi Stars Presents, Inc. and she has been the host of many of the television shows the company produces. "I can do my volunteer charity work because of Hawaiʻi Stars and my husband, Eddie Onouye, who is totally supportive of me!"

Feel the Beat of Aloha

Mick Fleetwood

Mick relaxing at home with Lyn and his daughters.

Having traveled all my life, putting roots down with my wife and children on Maui has given the sense of "coming home" a whole new meaning. That is aloha to me.

The rhythm of the aloha lifestyle not only resonates with the musician in me, but with my human desire to exchange love with all loving things.

Mick Fleetwood provides the beat behind Fleetwood Mac: he has been the man on the drums since 1968. When he is not on the road touring with the group, he returns to his home on Maui for a shot of aloha.

Hear Me, Island of Aloha

David B. Foellinger

Hear me Maui, island of aloha
Hear me Maui, island of my dreams
Sun and rainbows show the way to heaven
Radiant jewels rising from the sea.

Fill me with the passion of your fire
Move me with the magic of your wind
Soothe me in the coolness of your waters
Guide me with your light that shines within.

Listen as I pray with my eyes open
Grateful as a flower on a lei
Glowing with the spirit of aloha
Knowing that your power will not fade.

David is a songwriter. This song was submitted via the Practice Aloha website. www.PracticeAloha.org

My Aloha List

Al Nip

Aloha is letting a friend catch the best wave in the set.

Aloha is visiting your mom and dad as much as possible and letting them know that you appreciate everything they have done for you.

Aloha is planting Native Hawaiian plants, knowing that one day, your children's children will enjoy their beauty.

Aloha is caring that your children will practice good values and treat people with respect.

Aloha is playing that special song that a visitor requested, especially if it is Hawaiian.

Al has played music professionally on Maui since 1975, sharing the culture and history of the Islands through his "simple and sweet" songs. He retired after thirty-one years as an educator at Lahainaluna High School and currently teaches at the Kaunoa Senior Center in Lahaina.

Practice Aloha in a Parking Lot

Cecilio Rodriguez

Not long ago, I was driving into the parking lot of 'Āina Haina Shopping Center to go visit the Korean BBQ restaurant there. It was getting dark when I noticed a teenage boy leaning against a car and looking very, very bummed out.

I asked him what the trouble was and why he looked so forlorn. He said he didn't know what to do because he had borrowed his mom's car and locked the keys in it. He had been there for a while and, with no way to get into the car, he was thinking he would have to break the window! Of course, I asked why he didn't just call his mom and tell her what had happened. He said that not only was he locked out of the car, his phone was inside the vehicle. Yes, I could see it was on the front seat.

"Wow," I said, "that is a drag, but I'll tell you what today is...." He looked at me totally perplexed. "Today is your lucky day!"

I belong to AAA auto club, so I was allowed to have them come out and open a car—even someone else's car. I called and they promised to be there within forty-five minutes. I said to the boy, "Now, you can stop stressing and relax. The problem is solved."

Since the AAA member had to be on the scene when the tow truck arrived, we started talking story. He was so relieved, he thanked me over and over for helping him. "Wait, there are strings attached to this kindness," I said.

"Promise me the next time that you come upon someone who needs a helping hand—someone who needs groceries put into their car, or some mangoes picked for them, whatever—you will help them. That's how to say 'thank you' to me in the true sense."

I don't know if he helped someone else, but I'd like to think that he did. Maybe if he reads this he can let me know about his "Practice Aloha" moment. Helping someone else—even in an unlikely place such as a parking lot in 'Āina Haina—is the best way to spread the aloha.

Cecilio, an award-winning musician, was actually born and raised in Santa Barbara. He toured with Little Anthony and the Imperials before coming to Hawai'i. Half of the music duo Cecilio & Kapono he is also active with Easter Seals Hawai'i, hosting the annual telethon.

Born and Raised with Aloha

Kona Chang

Growing up here in the beautiful state of Hawai'i is really a blessing. I was born and raised in Waimānalo on the east side of O'ahu, where music and showing your aloha is part of the Hawaiian spirit.

Aloha is something each and every one of us who was brought into this world here in Hawai'i—or those who embrace the Hawaiian culture—bring out from within. I don't think it's something you learn, 'cause everyone on this planet has the ability to love, nurture, and give aloha not expecting anything in return!

For me, practicing and living aloha is very important. As a man who also believes in Jesus Christ who died for my sins and who is alive today, aloha is what God intended not only for Hawai'i, but for the entire world.

Kona is the youngest of seven, born into a family that embraced music. Imagine jamming on the beach with your cousin, Israel Kamakawiwo'ole!

Island Style

John Cruz

Refrain:

O n the island, we do it island style.
From the mountain to the ocean;
from the windward to the leeward side.
On the island, we do it island style.
From the mountain to the ocean;
from the windward to the leeward side.

Mama's in the kitchen cooking dinner
real nice
Beef stew on the stove, lomi salmon with the ice.
We eat and drink and we sing all day
Kanikapila* in the old Hawaiian way.

(Repeat refrain)

Wc go grandma's house on the weekend, clean yard
If we no go, grandma gotta work hard.
You know my grandma, she like the poi real sour
I love my grandma every minute, every hour.

(Repeat refrain 2 more times!)

John is a vocalist, guitarist, composer, and producer-and a Grammy winner!
Although born and raised in Hawai'i, John says he cut his musical teeth in
subways and bars in New York's Greenwich Village, as well as in the clubs in the
Boston area while attending the University of Massachusetts at Amherst.

---

* To play music together in Hawaiian. Singing usually accompanied by 'ukulele and/or
guitar. Definition from UrbanDictionary.com

The Story of the Lei

Barry Flanagan

For thousands of years, aloha has bonded all the different cultures and colors of Pacific Islanders to each other. That includes our new president.   He was raised near Mānoa Valley in Honolulu by his beloved grandmother, "Toot" (short for "Tūtū"). Yes, because he was born and raised here in Hawai'i, you could say President Barack Obama is a South Pacific Islander!

In an interesting parallel, my favorite Polynesian story is the story of the lei as a deep and profound symbol of love between child and grandparent. The word "pua" is the Hawaiian word for "flower." "Pua" is also the poetic word for "child" because Polynesians consider their children as beautiful and precious as their flowers.

In the story, the circle of a lei hanging from one's neck is beautifully symbolic. It visibly represents the arms of the grandchild around the neck of the grandparent. It is an unbreakable bond between the two generations.

The lei eloquently and beautifully expresses the unspoken, imperishable and perpetual wellspring of life and love. A lei is aloha represented.

According to the story, love represented by a lei can never be broken. Aloha is the unbreakable thread of the lei, the "tie that binds" all of Hawai'i's many different colored "pua"—flowers and children, young and old—together in one circle.

It tells us something. Aloha transcends all notions of nationality and culture.

Me ke aloha nui. (With lots of love)

Barry is the founder of the contemporary Hawaiian music duo HAPA. Born in New York City and raised in New Jersey, Barry came to the Hawaiian Islands in 1980 to study kī hōʻalu (slack-key guitar) and haku mele (poetic song composing). A prolific composer and performer, and one of Hawaiʻi's most respected and celebrated recording artists and producers, Barry has composed many of Hawaiʻi's most popular and cherished songs.

Inspiration from the Ancestors

Jay Larrin

"**A**cross the years, it has been my privilege to enter into meaningful, transformational friendships with many Hawaiian elders and island spiritual teachers who shared their interpretations about the true meaning of aloha. But imagine my amazement when one night, while entertaining at the piano in Waikiki's Sheraton Surfrider hotel, I looked up to see Hawai'i's great philosopher-poet-mystic, Pilahi Paki entering with the legendary singer and musician, Moe Keale!

Auntie Pilahi Paki had made a great impression on me when I heard her speak about "Aloha" at the very first Nā Hōkū Hanohano Awards. In her message that evening, she emphasized that aloha was the infinite, all-encompassing, all-loving gift to the allness of life, and that aloha emanated from the very Source of Love, the Creator of all life, and that aloha was for all races, all life. Aloha was the healing principle of unconditional love that could heal all who would practice its universal loving, healing principles. Her message was the highlight of that evening and her amazing presence made me wish that it would be possible for me to get to know her on a more personal level. Now it was truly wonderful to see Auntie Pilahi and Moe sit down at the table next to my piano!

Pilahi Paki was such a beautiful woman--regal, without a trace of arrogance. When it was time for my break, she motioned for me to join Moe and her at her table. It was such an honor to have her visit. Her "Aloha Chant" has been adopted by the Hawai'i State Legislature as the "Official Philosophy of the State of Hawai'i" and I had heard many reports of her spiritual work.

In our conversation that evening, Auntie Pilahi told me that she had brought Moe Keale with her, because she had written the words for a song that she wished to accompany her "Aloha Chant." She said that Moe had tried five times to compose a melody for her song, but that it had not worked out. She then said to me: "Last night in my dreams, my ancestors appeared to me and told me that you would write the melody for my song."

It was a bit daunting for me to agree to take on such a project, and it was a little surprising that this great Hawaiian legend would entrust me with such a task. But when she said that her ancestors had told her that I would be the one to write the music, it made me realize that there was no way to say "no" to Auntie Pilahi. Seeing my hesitation, she took my hand, lovingly patted it, and said, "Don't worry, my dear, all you have to do is say a little prayer, and you will receive the help you need to compose the music."

All I could say was, "Auntie, I will try." As she and Moe left the room that evening, I was both astonished and mystified...and a bit terrified that my efforts might fail her.

The next morning, I placed the hand-written words of her song, *Aloha Is,* on my piano. I set up a tape recorder next to me, and doing exactly as Auntie Pilahi had instructed, the words of a prayer unfolded. At the end of the prayer for Divine help, there came a deep feeling of what can only be described as peaceful exhilaration. With this inspiration, which came from being "in spirit" with her prayer, the project turned from being a task into a thing of joy!

I turned the tape recorder on, put my hands on the piano, and like a stream of pure, clear mountain water, the melody effortlessly flowed as I sang Auntie Pilahi's words of true aloha. In the singing of the song, from "out of the blue" came these words: "deep in the heart of Hawai'i." Auntie had said told me, "If other words come to you, please feel free to use them..." So I sang those words—after her words "It's tenderness and love"—to complete the line.

Upon singing the last note of *Aloha Is,* I turned the recorder off, reached for the phone, and called Auntie Pilahi. I asked her to listen to the recording to see if this was the direction in which she wanted the song to go. After the song ended, I asked her if she liked how things were progressing. On the other end of the line, there was a long, subdued silence. At the end of the silence I heard a sob....then a muffled little cry as she said: "My dear, do not change a thing!"

What a relief it was for me to know that she was pleased! She thanked me profusely, and I thanked her for her words that she had so lovingly shared. About two years later, Moe Keale recorded the album *Aloha Is a Part of Me, a Part of You* and included his ethereal interpretation of *Aloha Is.* In 1987, it won the Nā Hōkū Hanohano award as Hawai'i's song of the year."

Here is a poem written by Jay Larrin for the Moloka'i Ho'e" the annual canoe race from Moloka'i to Oahu.

In the Harbors of Heaven

Here in these islands we live in the abandonment of time
We are blessed with cooling forests and shadowed mountains
We are soothed by healing streams of sacred valleys
We dwell in the harbors of heaven.

Beneath the sun there is only one Hawaii,
And her people are the treasure of paradise,
The children of Aloha who know the pathways of the ocean,
Gentle friends with loving eyes.

This is the realm of the wonders of the sea
Our hearts are united in serenity.

Our souls are filled with the beauty of her songs,
The songs of old Hawaii.

This is a world of sea dreamers, breeze drifters, and riders of the
wind.
The stars shine for those who free their hearts,
And choose to live in love as friends.

Here in these islands we live in the abandonment of time.
We dwell in the harbors of heaven.

Jay has composed many of Hawai'i's best loved songs including The Snows
of Mauna Kea and Moloka'i Lullaby. Originally from Tennessee, he is a world
traveler and now lives on Oahu.

Practicing Aloha Song

Cindy Paulos

Here Cindy Paulos shows her love of music and Hawai'i with a song she wrote about aloha. The song is featured as a music video on the Practice Aloha website.

Rainbows bless these Islands,
where Heaven touches land.
The Light that's in the People's Eyes,
shows love is in command.
The scent of ginger and plumeria fills the air,
and the blessing of Beauty is everywhere.
Look into our Heart and Soul,
and see how much we care.
Practicing Aloha ... each and every day ...
We're guided by Aloha and kindness shows the way.
Practicing Aloha with the Spirit of these lands,
Practicing Aloha brings peace into our hands.
Rushing mountain waters,
light the streams to distant shores.
Keiki play and laugh on the beach,
our hearts call out for more.
This is a sacred 'aina, that we cherish and we share.
The magic that we find here, is what we all look for.
Practicing Aloha ... each and every day,
The Spirit that's alive here, guides us on our way.
Remember that aloha—the breath of Spirit—lives
There's love in the Aloha... It's a blessing that we give.

Cindy has been a familiar voice on local radio for years, but not everyone knows she is also a minister. She produced Practice Aloha radio spots that are heard on local radio featuring uplifting stories by some of the folks in this book.

A Philosophical Gift of Thanks

Willie K
(Willie Kahaiali'i)

The gift of breath, though taken for granted, is recognized as we live and breathe each day. When we are awake, or asleep, we honor its presence as an everyday duty. We pay no attention, nor mind, nor even question its great work. Yet it is there, supplying our bodies with an energetic rhythm, beating in between each moment of passing time.

When life is placed on the stage of being, our very existence becomes the major headline. Our first cry, our first tear, our first gasp of excitement! Now born, in the first act we display curiosity. Our story then continues on until the knowledge of our own existence becomes refreshing.

How beautiful God must be to have patience in creating me.

Willie-he performs as Willie K-is known for his masterful blending of many styles of music including Hawaiian, R&B, and jazz. He is also president of Hui o Waa Kaulua, a nonprofit organization about the canoe.

Aloha in an Old Hawaiian Song

Eric Gilliom and Joel Clark Kira

This song is from the CD *Like Chow Fun*. It speaks to the very idea that the Spirit of Aloha is preserved in old Hawaiian songs.

Old Hawaiian Songs
Words and Music by Eric Gilliom and Joel Clark Kira

Winters come
The storms are blowing in again
Summer fades to the sound of falling rain
Golden days gone by
Hawai'i calls … E komo mai (welcome)
The spirit of aloha lives on
In old Hawaiian songs

Stories told … Legends from days of old
Memories we will always hold
In the heart of these Isle
Hawai'i calls … E komo mai
The spirit of aloha lives on
In old Hawaiian songs

Happy to sing
They bring a tear to the eye
And a smile

Well here we are
Living in these modern days
Dreams are made every time we play
Wishes from way back when
Hawai'i calls … E komo mai
The spirit of aloha lives on
In old Hawaiian songs, Old Hawaiian songs … Old Hawaiian
    songs.

Eric and Joel spent many days and nights listening to Eric's grandmother, Jennie Hanaialii Kaahanui Woodd, sing the old-style songs. They wrote this in honor of her and all the kūpuna.

Waimea

Bla Pahinui

Waimea, Oh—so high,
Wai, mea, mountains high.
You're like, the wind , that blows,
beneath the skies.
Waimea, I'm in love with you.
Wai, mea, Oh—so high,
Wai, mea, Oh—so shy.
From mauka to makai,
and the cold winds blow
beneath the skies.
Waimea, I'm in love with you.
I'm staring at the moon,
gazing at the stars
and feeling, all of you.
'Cause one day I'll be gone
leaving you a song
of love and peace,
and beauty is what you are.
Waimea, I'm in love with you.

Bla started playing music at the age of ten when his Dad bought him a Martin 'ukulele. He joined the family onstage soon after and has been performing ever since. Bla "James" is the son of the legendary Hawaiian slack-key guitar player Philip "Gabby" Pahinui.

Aloha Begins with the Music

Jimmy Borges

Aloha is when I'm singing and the orchestra and the audience becomes one in movement and feeling. It gathers every positive emotion within my heart, and I am reaching out and embracing another spirit.

Aloha is also allowing others to express their own feelings without judgment.

Aloha is being truthful—under all conditions and circumstances.

Aloha is the attempt to make the life of everyone you meet a little bit better because you "touched" them.

Me ke aloha pumehana … mālama pono
(With warm affection…take care)

Jimmy is a musician and an actor. You may remember him from Magnum P.I. and of course Hawaii Five-O!

A Light

Jim "Kimo" West

Aloha is the unconditional love and respect for our fellow man and for all living and non-living things, for our ancestors, our children, for the air we breathe, and the land we walk upon.

Aloha is what we find when we can ignore all our fears and desires. It is the light that shines eternally from the jewel deep inside us.

Kimo is a musician, slack-key guitarist, and composer. In addition to Hawaiian music, he works with "Weird Al" Yankovic.

Ahhhh-Looow-Haaaa

Danny Kaleikini

I believe that Aloha is the breath of life and love that we share with each other.

"Aloha ke kahi. I ke kahi": Love one another.

"Aloha ke akua": God is Love— God is Aloha

Danny has a video on the Practice Aloha website. Go to www.PracticeAloha.org to hear his trademark style of saying-or is it singing-ALOHA!

Aloha is a Butterfly

Nohelani Cypriano

The first thing I thought of to express what Aloha means to me, was my mom, Leinaʻala Simerson. She was a longtime and respected Hawaiian entertainer who passed away from ovarian cancer on January 8, 2000.

She lived aloha and gave it unconditionally and lovingly to everyone who knew her. I always remember my mother saying "yes" to everyone. If someone needed help, my mom would be there. If you needed someone to sing at a family lūʻau, birthday party, anything … my mom would say yes! Needed a place to stay? My mom would welcome you. Needed hundreds of party favors? My mom made them for you, no charge. She was always there for everyone, always ready to listen and to give.

When she passed away, we held her Celebration of Life service. I truly had no idea how many people she had touched until then. All day hundreds of people came to sing, share stories, and pay their respect to a wonderful, generous soul.

She continues to give to this day—a beautiful pulelehua (butterfly) sign whenever I need her. My mother not only Practiced Aloha in life and in her passing—I am sure this Hawaiian soul was a gift from the Heavens. She lived aloha to its fullest.

Nohelani is a versatile performer—a vocalist, keyboard player, and composer. Her recent CD, *Pulelehua (My Precious Butterfly)*, is dedicated to her mother.

Aloha Indeed

Ried Kapo Ku

So, now with all this talk about aloha you might be expecting an "Aloooooooha!" Well, this homey don't play that.

See, that's kind of a Waikīkī lūʻau thing. I'm gonna teach you a real cool way to greet someone in Hawaiian starting with this word "aloha" as taught to me by such awesome people as Haunani Bernadino, Grandma Ku, Mikaʻele Bito, Kaleo Oyama, Kamanō Lammano, and Kamanu Bird.

Yes, the word "aloha" is used as a greeting for "hello" and "goodbye" but, more importantly, it means "love" of the most unconditional sort. In my awareness, aloha also incorporates the ideas of respect, kindness, compassion, understanding, balance, harmony, connection, tranquility, generosity, tenderness, joy, and just about any warm fuzzy word of the sort.

When you greet someone with aloha what you're really saying is "let this energy of aloha connect us, flow between us, within us and around us, and guide our interaction." When you use it as "goodbye" you're really saying "let this energy of aloha go with you to protect you."

So, with this understanding I'm going to offer my aloha to you and you can simply, respond with "Aloha nō." This nō is not the English "no" which means "not." It is the Hawaiian "nō" giving emphasis to the preceding word. Sort of "aloha indeed."

You ready? Aloha iā ʻoukou—Aloha to all of you ...ʻo ke aloha wale nō. Very cool. And by the way, aloha isn't the exclusive property of Hawaiians. All cultures, I believe, have the same concept in one form or another. Call it love, the true self, spiritual consciousness/awareness, Ke Akua, or God if you like. Heck, realize it in yourself.

We are all one and the same spiritual goop!

Ried is a musician who is thoroughly Hawaiian, but most folks don't know he was born in Oregon! He combines music, meditation, and yoga for his own style of Practicing Aloha in his life.

Practice Aloha
Around the World

You don't have to live in Hawai'i—or even be Hawaiian—to embrace the Aloha Spirit.

Aloha can be found in the most surprising places at the most unlikely times. You just have to have an open heart and mind to recognize it!

The stories in this chapter prove there is room for aloha anywhere on earth.

Global Aloha

Ateeka

In the northern European winter, darkness descends upon the streets shortly after tea-time and the nights are long. The few hours of winter sunlight that do exist are often obscured by a thick pasting of clouds often bursting with icy rain. Trees are bare and city folk heavily clothed to keep out the chill. Eyes cast towards the ground or hidden under a wide umbrella, the northern city populations seem to be introverted and as frosty as their weather. Does Aloha exist even here?

As is often a typical story heard on in the Islands, I arrived in Maui in 1993 on vacation and literally "never went home." Maui became more "home" for me than any other place I had lived before, including my birthplace on the mainland. I immersed myself into the solar Lahaina community, nourished myself with its loving support, and gave back in whatever ways I could.

As fate would have it, in 2005 I met an extraordinary human being who happened to be a charming Italian from Milano. This man was destined to be my future husband. After a long courtship and countless flights between the tropics of Maui and the fashion capital of Italy, we decided I would move to Italy and we would build our life together there.

After the initial excitement of moving to a new city and starting a new life had quieted down, I began to notice a sense of "something missing." I was perplexed and melancholy. I couldn't be missing the sunshine. Italian summers have the best climate of almost anywhere in the world. I couldn't be missing the sea, because we often took the short train ride to the Ligurian coast to swim in the salty Mediterranean waters. It certainly couldn't be companionship. I was (and still am) in love with an adventurous, affectionate, and radiantly positive man. I was stumped. What was it that felt different in my heart?

One day, I was overwhelmed with a realization that what I was missing was aloha—that rare combination of connection and kindness that was so much a part of my life in Hawai'i. Aloha is spontaneous generosity of personal energy, of time, of resources. Aloha is a trust in the flow of life to bring to us just what we need for ourselves and our communities. In this, we are able to give freely, whether it be a wide toothy smile, a helping hand, a shoulder to cry on. Aloha is the willingness to make contact—eye contact and human contact. I had taken the Spirit of Aloha for granted all of my time on Maui.

That was it! It was the lack of human connection in a big city packed with humans. I had a sense of malnourishment. All the best pasta and wines and cheeses couldn't fill my hunger for spontaneous, loving human exchange. I had succumbed to the local cultural patterns of turning my gaze to the ground and staying "to myself" as the others did. I had somehow melded in with the faster rhythms of the city, tempos that rarely left you the time to say "good morning" or to chat with the cashier at the store, or to give assistance to one who needed a hand. I had allowed my Spirit of Aloha to be subdued!

So from that day on, I decided that whether here in the city, or traveling around the world, my "mission" would be to Practice Global Aloha (Globaloha)!

For a few years now, I have been interweaving the word "aloha" brightly into my developing Italian vocabulary. I have slowed back down to an Island rhythm, even here in the city. I have learned that almost nothing is worth rushing. I take the chance and look into the eyes of strangers with a smile and say "Buon giorno!" Some are shocked to be addressed, look to the ground and walk on faster. I accept this with patience. However, most are pleasantly surprised with my attempt to connect and respond with a smile. Frequently, a conversation is started, and we share a simple human moment. This is what the soul craves: simple, mutual human exchanges of kindness. The soul is nourished by aloha.

I have learned that the Spirit of Aloha resides within each one of us, no matter our nationalities, creeds, or belief systems. Human loving kindness and acknowledgement is aloha, and it dwells in all human hearts. It is not difficult to find; we simply need to slow down, perceive more, and be courageous enough to open our hearts to others.

When we awaken aloha in ourselves, we help to awaken it in others. A change toward a non-violent united humanity is at hand!

So, I encourage you, wherever you are. Close your eyes for a moment, slow down, and feel your heart beat. Breathe in a memory of the unmistakable scent of Hawaiian tradewinds. Let this memory transport you to the birthplace of aloha. As you exhale, let the tradewind of your heart gently expand around the world … carrying the vibration of aloha to whomever it breezes past.   Practice Global Aloha.

Ateeka's story was submitted via the Practice Aloha website—possibly from Italy!

One Mind

Lola Milani

A ll peoples know aloha.
I was raised with shalom, my husband salaam.

Love, greeting, welcome, honoring the divine within.

This being called human has one mind, same wiring, same needs, same water, same blood, breathes the same air, feels the same wind, hears the same heartbeat, births the same child, dies the same death.

One person endlessly repeating: aloha.

Story submitted via the Practice Aloha website. www.PracticeAloha.org

The Aloha/Shalom Connection

Emil Richards

The first time I heard about Hawai'i was in 1941 when I was nine years old. I was coming out of a movie with my brother and it was snowing in Hartford, Connecticut. There was a man on the corner selling the Sunday paper yelling "Extra! Read all about it. Japanese bomb Pearl Harbor." I didn't know where Pearl Harbor, Hawai'i, was until that day.

The first time I went to Hawai'i I was twenty-four years old. It was 1954. I heard people saying aloha, but didn't understand it very well.

I was (and still am) a studio recording musician and a player of jazz. When I was thirty years old, I went around the world as a musician accompanying Frank Sinatra with a six-man combo. We went to Israel on that concert tour and traveled all over the country for five days.

Israel had recently obtained its statehood. The joy and happiness felt there at that time is what it must have been like in 1776 when America first got its independence!

Every one went around saying shalom to each other. The amazing love that was felt truly opened my heart abundantly.

When my wife Celeste and I returned to Hawai'i in 1970 we heard the word "aloha" again. That's when we realized that "aloha" was a lot like "shalom." It is a way for people to greet each other with a strong feeling of love and kindness.

We have met so many wonderful friends in the Islands and always feel that wonderful feeling of aloha when we are here at our second home. I have one of the Practice Aloha bumper stickers on my car. It is a good reminder of this wonderful place and the practice of aloha.

Emil Richards is an internationally celebrated jazz and studio musician who has worked with Joni Mitchell, Frank Zappa, The Beach Boys, Ella Fitzgerald, Marvin Gaye, and George Harrison. He has played on two thousand film and television show scores!

Been Around the World, Found the Aloha

Jack Fisher

I have come to accept that there is a mysterious force (perhaps mana) that draws us all to this remote pinpoint in a vast ocean. Many times over the past thirty-four years I have asked myself a recurring question: Why am I here? Why Hawai'i, when I've traveled and seen a good portion of this planet?

I've come up with some of the more obvious answers. The multitude of micro-climates. The ocean. The dormant volcano. The people. The relaxed lifestyle. Aloha and 'ohana and 'āina. The prospect of dancing to the beat of a far different drum. The fact that we can enjoy the rights and privileges of American citizenship far from the mainland madding crowd! However, it goes deeper.

I refer to my racial makeup as "European poi dog." The blood of Sicily, Turkey, Sweden, and Russia flows in my veins. My parents, one a Jew and one a Roman Catholic, rebelled against the "old ways" of their immigrant parents, who arrived in early twentieth-century America through the portals of Ellis Island.

We, their children, were raised bereft of our cultural heritage, adrift in a vast sea of humanity with no anchor and no compass. My father was a military man, so we traveled the length and breadth of the nation in my youth. Our lives and my father's career were dictated by the U.S. Air Force. We lived, in the best of times, on the edge of poverty. A family of six was hard-pressed to live on the salary of a junior military officer in post-war America.

When I was three years old, we arrived in Hawai'i. It was 1946, immediately after the great tsunami. We lived for seven years in military housing at Hickam Air Force Base on the island of O'ahu. My brother was born at Tripler Army Hospital in 1951.

My mother was outgoing, gregarious, and a talented musician, and soon had many friends in the Hawaiian community that worked in and around the military installations. She learned the hula. "Studied hula," she would correct. "You can never learn it all; the best you can do is study."

I learned to swim at the old Natatorium, and ventured into the ocean swells in front of the Royal Hawaiian Hotel for the first time while hanging on my mother's neck. I ate shave ice while sitting on the backs of the ancient tortoises that cropped grass in what is now Kapi'olani Park.

In my early thirties, I came to Maui for a two-week vacation, and never left. In thirty-four years I have visited the mainland five times, the last time in 1991. I gave up many things that seemed so important to me in my earlier life: museums, art galleries, the stage, and the ability to jump in a vehicle and drive for days on end.

Somehow, those things recede into the background when the tradewinds are blowing, the tropical sun warms the blood, and the waves are lapping at your feet.

I lived my childhood in two- and three-year stints in Roswell, Boise, Elyria, Salina, Stockton, Memphis, Buena Park, Lampasas, Dundalk, Phoenix, and Jamestown. I attended seventeen schools in twelve years. In my early twenties there were life experiences in London, Ostend, the Zugzspitz, Naples, San Juan, Panama Canal Zone, San Jose, Caracas, Bogota, and Washington, D.C.

Then I returned to Hawai'i Nei in the early '70s, this time to the island of Maui. I felt for the first time the true meaning of "home" and I knew in my heart of hearts that this was a permanent bond with the concept of "Aloha 'āina," love of the land.

Jack can be found either practicing yoga or at his company, Jack Fisher Realty, on Maui.

Aloha Around Town

Carolyn Classen

PRACTICE ALOHA™
Maui, Hawaii

I just saw a bumper sticker in town saying "Practice Aloha." So I blogged about spreading the Aloha Spirit in April and August of this year. Here's my final update for 2008.

Aloha Spirit is that special extension of extra kindness and thoughtfulness we see exhibited in Hawai'i, but it can be found anywhere in the world. For instance, I came across a server at a lunch counter who realized I was thirty-five cents short on my lunch order. I only had a ten-dollar bill in my wallet and couldn't pay for that Thai chicken salad and apple/guava juice I had ordered! She smiled and said, "No problem." She took the balance out of the tip jar. Now that was true Aloha Spirit and great customer relations.

Then a clerk at a drug store was kind enough to give me a Hawai'i state quarter when I asked for one, saying that she could easily get another. But the one she gave me was the one she had saved for herself. That was Aloha Spirit and I told her so.

A number of patrons in the Pima County public library branches have been very gracious. Two people on separate occasions have noticed that I needed to use the internet on one of the computers, and voluntarily informed me when they were done in order that I could use their computer, and not waste more time waiting. How thoughtful of them, in a world where most people hardly interact with each other.

Carolyn Classen was born and raised on the Big Island. She is a former practicing attorney and now a citizen journalist/blogger. She has two short stories in Rick Carroll's The Best of Hawai'i's Best Spooky Tales. Carolyn blogged on Tucsoncitizen.com on December 11, 2008, about a Practice Aloha sticker she saw near her home in Arizona. That was our first clue that the message was spreading beyond Hawai'i.

No Place Like Hawai'i

Kutmaster Spaz

I have traveled all over the world for my career as a DJ. No matter where I go, I find the best part of the trip is coming home to Hawai'i.

I always tell people that here in Hawai'i we have one thing the rest of the world doesn't, and that's the Aloha Spirit. Aloha to me is a mutual friendly smile when you see someone on the street, or a hello wave back to some one who waves at you (even if you have no idea who they are). It's the love that is put into the preparation of our Island food, the passion put into the local music, or a shaka (thank you) when a car lets you cut into their lane on the freeway.

Aloha is the warm feeling you get when you meet someone that is so humble you know that they would give the shirt off their back, the food off their plate, and last dollar in their pocket to help a person out (even if they have never met the person before).

That is aloha to me, and even if we are not in Hawai'i, it is something we should be practicing every day.

Kutmaster is a DJ and nationally recognized re-mixer by the music industry. He is the producer and host of the local television show DIS-N-DAT.

Practice Aloha
On the Job

We spend a good percentage of our lives at work. Shouldn't it be the best time of the day? For many of us here in the Islands, it truly is!

Working and Practicing Aloha are not mutually exclusive. Think of it as multi-tasking put to its highest and best use.

These stories show how a little aloha goes a long way during the workday ...

Living Aloha with the Rainbow Wāhine

Dana Takahara-Dias

Success is a journey, not a destination, and I have been fortunate to have had many journeys thus far in my life. The paths have been varied to say the least, but a common denominator has been constant: I have tried my best to live aloha.

Aloha means many things to many people; however, for me it is simply this: Giving more than is expected and doing it cheerfully and with genuine warmth and sincerity.

My new journey involves me returning to the University of Hawai'i where I now give back to a program that has given so much to me. I find myself in a most wondrous place as the new head coach of the Rainbow Wāhine basketball team. As a proud alumna and former Wāhine basketball player, I am reminded each and every day to live aloha.

We are ambassadors and we hope to bring great excitement, success and pride to the University and state of Hawai'i. Our Rainbow Wāhine basketball program preaches and lives by these core values:

Respect: With such cultural diversity in our Islands, we respect all people, cultures, ideals, and opinions.

Achievement: We set the bar high by setting high standards and living them every day. Lead by example.

Improvement: Maintaining the status quo is not an option; we continue to learn, grow, and improve daily.

Nurture: Emphasize your core values by nurturing your mind, body, and soul.

Blessings: Count and appreciate your blessings, no matter how big or how small.

'Ohana: Take care of one another and love unconditionally.

Winning: Win with grace and lose with dignity.

Work: Plan the work and work the plan. Do what you love doing and it will never be considered work.

Advocate healthy habits and live a wholesome lifestyle.

Humble: Practice humility and be humble about your accomplishments and achievements.

Important: It is nice to be important but more important to be nice.

Never let an opportunity go by without saying thank you or please.

Enthusiasm: Nothing great is ever accomplished without enthusiasm. Enthusiasm and a positive attitude are contagious!

Dana is the first female head coach at the University of Hawai'i since 1979. Her story not only spells out what it means to Practice Aloha, we think it would make a great cheer at a Rainbow Wāhine basketball game!

Words of Aloha

Lisa Chappel

Practicing Aloha is being …
    … kind and giving,
  … caring and sharing,
  … grateful, compassionate, charitable, forgiving, and loving.

Practicing Aloha is being …
    … respectful to the beautiful island on which we are blessed to live.

Lisa is general manager of Māla Ocean Tavern. Although she travels a bit to the mainland, Lisa has lived on and off on Maui since 1975.

Isles of Smiles

Tony Novak-Clifford

Maybe it is because I am a photographer, but one of the first things I notice when visiting a place for the first time is whether or not the people I meet are smiling. That is the thing that stands out most in my mind about my first encounter with the island of Maui, an island where I have been privileged enough to have remained a guest for almost thirty years now.

People smile here. Okay, people may smile everywhere, from time to time. At least their lips curl up on each end. People in the Islands, however, seem to have this perpetual grin that is ear-to-ear big—teeth-flashing big—deep from every fiber of their being big. It's as contagious as it is disarming, I'll have you know.

I admit that I didn't quite know what to make of it at first. It threw me off. Here I was fresh off the boat from the East Coast, a place where people you pass on the street seem as grey and stern as the weather three-quarters of the year. To suddenly arrive on the shores of a tropical island with mountains sharp, angular, and green; surrounded by water the color of precious gemstones; and breezes scented with plumeria was already an amazing transition for an uninitiated new arrival like myself. It all seemed so exotic and completely foreign to me.

And then there were these people…these amazing people. They were big and beautiful; they were brown and golden; and they were smiling! Well, not so much a smile as it was a giant opening in the face, roughly where the mouth should be, curled in an upward direction on each end. A smile like that can swallow you whole and then spit you out again a new man (or woman, as the case may be). And that's exactly what happened to me.

The first time one of those big brown faces reached out and took my small, pale hand into their giant brown hands, clamping ever so gently, so warmly, in a gesture of welcome, the giant, tooth-filled grin spreading from ear to ear, I was immediately besotted—a complete goner.

The weather, the scenery, the sensual surrounding sea—these things alone were enough to make me linger in these Islands for a while. But it has been the people that have made me want to stay here forever.

After arriving in the Islands, I had to look for things like a job, a place to live, a bed, a bicycle, or car. I remember going from shop to shop on Front Street in Lahaina looking for work, inquiring about rentals and some of the other creature comforts one is forced to leave behind when flying to an island on the other side of the world. I remember those shopkeepers; some of them remain friends to this day.

If they didn't have a job available or one of the other things I had inquired about, they picked up a telephone to call an auntie, a cousin, or a friend. Speaking into the receiver in that exotic, sing-song dialect we call pidgin, they would ask the person on the other end: "I get one malahini haole boy heah. You get one bed you like sell?" Or maybe a bicycle or an 'ohana cottage for rent. What I remember most is that they took the time, without giving it a second thought, to extend kindness to a stranger. That kindness always came bundled with one of those enormous smiles.

You can call that aloha. No other word, in my mind, comes close to encompassing the feeling one gets from just hearing the word. Certainly no other terms sounds as magical and musical. Aloha!

Several notable Hawaiian authorities have lent their knowledge on the subject of aloha to this book. I am neither Hawaiian nor a scholar.

I am only an observer and a guest. When I first washed ashore, I was armed with a very basic knowledge of Hawai'i, its people, practices, and culture (and most of that garnered from the Michener novel). It was the feeling of immediate, almost unconditional acceptance of those that I encountered and continue to encounter that were my first experiences with what I will call aloha. Their sharing of backyard fruit or fish or game, their invitations to join them under dusty carports to strum along to impromptu chang-a-lang music sessions and the ubiquitous passing of cold beer and fresh poke.… In my experience these are not everyday occurrences in most places. And then there were those smiles—always those smiles.

Though the scholars may disagree on certain points, these are the things that have come to define aloha for me. Aloha is a spoken embrace and a bestowing of love. It is a sense of warmth and an acknowledgement of family that reaches beyond bloodlines. It comes, always, wrapped in one of those heroic smiles.

Tony is a commercial and editorial photographer living on the island of Maui. He is grateful for the opportunity to Practice Aloha by lending his talents and Photoshop® software to the photo-editing of this book.

It Takes a Village ...
to Build a Business

Lani Medina Weigert

Growing up in Kailua, Oʻahu, I watched as our neighbors shared fish, mangoes, chickens, and whatever they had with one another. Money was tight, but we managed and we were happy. We looked out for each other and even scolded neighbors' kids saying, "Get home before I call your mada!" Those truly were the "good old days." We always helped each other and waved "hello" whenever we saw one another. It was a simple life, one that wasn't always easy, but was rich in character.

Today, as the co-owner of the Kula Maui Lavender Farm in Upcountry Maui, I see the economy struggling, and any business can be very uncertain. But when I recall the "old days," it is easy to see what is different. Back then we did not compete with one another. Instead we included and embraced each other. In my own business, I place aloha as my "value center" and I include, rather than exclude, it when it comes to my dealings in the business community.

Aloha means love, friendship, and responsibility to me. I look to my neighbors in business and embrace them. I give them our lavender and they make whatever it is that they are experts in, such as jellies, chocolates, soaps, candles and more. This way, I don't compete with them. Instead, they become my partner.

This Practicing Aloha in business results in abundance for all of us. To this day, I still practice the old adage with a slight twist: It takes a village ... to raise a business!

Lani is co-owner of Kula Maui Lavender Farm. She co-wrote a book *The Maui Book of Lavender* with her business partner Alii Chang.

Aloha Through the Ulupono Initiative

Kyle Datta

In my job at Ulupono Initiative, we are working to create a more sustainable future for Hawaiʻi's next generation by investing in local agriculture, renewable energy, and waste management. We have the honor and pleasure of working with individuals and organizations, big and small, that are contributing to positive change in Hawaiʻi. Each and every day we are truly amazed at the depth of commitment from these organizations and individuals, whom we see as Hawaiʻi's future leaders.

Yet we know that these organizations cannot provide for the community without the help and support of all. Every individual—our friends, neighbors, and loved ones—has the power to make a difference. For our family, Practicing Aloha means living mindfully, consistent with the values of aloha. It means understanding that our individual actions can make a difference in helping our community.

When my family sits down to eat, we enjoy foods that come from local farmers, fishermen, and ranchers. We are careful to use energy efficiently and obtain as much energy as we can from the sun, contributing to our state's sustainability.

It is our sincere hope that our family's choices contribute to making our society more secure and resilient. We hope yours will too.

Ulupono Initiative was founded by eBay founder Pierre Omidyar and his wife Pam who now live in Hawaiʻi. Kyle and partner Robin Campaniano bring impressive professional backgrounds to this social investment firm dedicated to improving the quality of life for Hawaiʻi's residents through sustainability.

Whalewatching with "The Greatest"

Greg Kaufman

During the last three decades I have had some incredible whale experiences at Pacific Whale Foundation. People always ask me "what was the best whale-watching experience you ever had?" Having spent thousands of hours on the ocean in the presence of whales, it really is hard to choose just one to single out as "the greatest" whale experience.

However, it is really my shared experiences whale-watching that I recall most fondly. In 1981, when we were a fledgling organization, 112 fourth graders from Kīhei Elementary School raised $3,800 (all in quarters!) for our research efforts. That whale-watch from Māʻalaea Harbor with those kids (whose kids are now adults) will forever live fresh in my memory.

Last evening, *Ocean Voyager's* sunset whale-watch was another poignant reminder. It was a perfect evening for a whale-watch: light winds, clear skies, calm seas, plenty of whales, a perfect sunset, and a glorious full moon. A picture-perfect whale-watch experienced by myself and ninety-two other passengers, including "The Greatest," Muhammad Ali, and his dear friend, singer, songwriter, and actor Kris Kristofferson.

When I was nine years old and glued to the radio, I cheered wildly as Ali upset Sonny Liston to win the world heavyweight championship at age twenty-two. "I shook up the world! I shook up the world!" Ali shouted after winning. I can recall the "Fight of the Century," where he lost to Fraser, the "Rumble in the Jungle" with Foreman, the "Thrilla in Manila" rematch with Fraser, and his loss and then subsequent win over Spinks to become the three-time heavyweight boxing champ. All legendary and exemplary of what an amazing athlete Ali was.

But where Ali left an indelible mark on me was when he fought with his words and not his fists. He was a conscientious objector to the Vietnam War, saying "I ain't got no quarrel with them Viet Cong." He was found guilty of refusing induction into the armed forces by the U.S. Department of Justice. His passport was revoked and he was stripped of his boxing association title.

Despite this imposed hardship he remained steadfast, and focused his efforts instead on religious and humanitarian issues.

In June 1971, the U.S. Supreme Court found that his objection to the draft was justifiable based on his religious beliefs, and overturned Ali's conviction. I recall feeling emboldened by his actions: you can stand for what you believe in—and win.

Now one of the most recognizable individuals in the world, he used his notoriety to foster good for others. Traveling across continents, he has hand-delivered food and medical supplies to children in Cote D'Ivoire, Indonesia, Mexico, and Morocco, among other countries.

In 2005 he received the Presidential Medal of Freedom and the United Nations recognized him as a Messenger of Peace from 1998 to 2008 for his work in developing nations. He was also on hand to meet Nelson Mandela upon his release from prison.

And last night I had the opportunity to show "The Greatest," Muhammad Ali, whales for the first time in his life. In fact, we were told this was to be Ali's first venture on to the ocean on a boat to view any form of marine life.

What a show it was! A mother, calf, and escort slowly approached *Ocean Voyager* and glided gracefully along our starboard side. With Muhammad standing at the rail, the newborn calf repeatedly raised its pectoral fins and fanned the evening air, as if to bid "aloha" to all onboard. In all we observed eight different pods, all lolling about in a becalmed Māʻalaea Bay. As we headed to port, seven whales emerged in the streaking moonlight cast upon the water's surface, with a full moon emerging in the sky.

After the passengers disembarked I was invited to sit with Muhammad, chat, and take photos. I gave him a copy of my book *Hawai'i's Humpback Whales: The Long Journey Back,* which fascinated him.

Sitting beside him, I felt the need to confess my admiration. I leaned closed to him and said: "I know you may have heard this many times before, but I want to let you know that watching you box was magical. But it was your quick wit and your willingness to fight with your words and do good with your fame that has been an inspiration to me. Thank you."

Despite Ali's battle with Parkinson's, he turned to me, lifted his head, and placed his face close to mine, our noses nearly touching. His eyes lit up as he stared into me. For a moment I felt frozen in time: I was seeing the same Ali glare that Liston, Fraser, Foreman, and Spinks endured. Then his eyes softened and a smile broke on his face, just like when he used to riff with the late Howard Cossell, and he raised his hand and offered to shake my hand in gratitude.

As we escorted him to his car, he asked for my book to read after he was buckled in, and began patiently turning the pages and carefully examining the photos and illustrations. "He listened to every word you said today during your narration of the whale-watch. He really enjoyed himself. This is something he will never forget," Mr. Kristofferson said.

Nor will I.

Greg is the founder and chairman of the board of the Pacific Whale Foundation. Over the past thirty years, Pacific Whale Foundation has taught more than three million people about the ocean through educational whale-watching, and ocean ecotourism programs.

You and Eye Contact

Larry Feinberg

On Maui people acknowledge your presence with eye contact and a smile. The warmth of a smile means "aloha" to me.

Larry Feinberg has been a real estate agent on Maui for twenty-five years.

Practicing Mahalo, Too

Mayor Mufi Hannemann

One of my maxims of leadership is this: Practice the Mahalo Principle; thank someone every day. It's just the other side of the Practicing Aloha coin.

We often take for granted our spouses, children, and those closest to us, failing to reciprocate their love and acceptance.

We walk past the police officer or the custodian without acknowledging the good deeds they do for us. We don't fully appreciate the beauty of this land, the bounty of this world, and the aloha of our people, as we neglect to return this generosity through our contributions to their perpetuity.

We should each Practice the Mahalo Principle, as we do with aloha, by thanking those around us every day for their love and sacrifices, and by striving to leave this a better place than we found it.

Mayor Hannemann is Honolulu-born, Harvard-educated, and an alumnus of 'Iolani School. In addition to serving as Honolulu's mayor, he served in the Carter, Reagan, Clinton, and Bush administrations in a number of appointed capacities.

Red Saturn

Dawn Kawahara

I had traveled to Kailua, Oʻahu, for a business meeting, making my way over the Pali in my rental car. Feeling sure I could find my way back, I pulled out of my company's parking lot at twilight, expecting to see the freeway signs that would direct me back toward Honolulu. Somehow my sense of direction had become skewed, and I found myself in an area I didn't recognize.

I tried another tack, but this one didn't work, either. Night had fallen, and I started feeling nervous. The dashboard clock was ticking away. I realized I had lost my buffer time and still had to turn in my rental car before check-in. My flight was the last one to Kauaʻi for the evening. It was time to act.

The brightly lit windows of a local hamburger fast food restaurant called, so I drove toward it. I parked in the lot and hurried in to ask one of the local residents to redirect me.

A woman sitting with a young girl looked friendly, so I approached them. Excusing myself, I explained my situation. The woman agreed that "getting out of Kailua" could be tricky. She pulled a small pad out of her purse and proceeded to draw me a map, showing one-way streets and a junction.

"There's our order," said the girl, going to the counter.

"My daughter," said the woman smiling. Then she focused on the directional arrows she had drawn and asked if her map was understandable. They were unwrapping their hamburgers as I thanked her and hurried out the door.

The directions were good. I stopped for a red light before entering the freeway ramp, then noticed a car behind me flashing its lights. Turning around, I saw it was the same woman with her daughter. She stuck her head out of the window, calling out, "Go! We're going to follow you to make sure."

The light turned, and I was off and running, their car escorting me all the way up and over the Pali. Now I was well on track and expected them to double back, but the car stayed on my tail. As I angled off to Nimitz Highway, they peeled by with a couple of aloha toots of the horn. My mirror reflected their bright red Saturn—as red as any heart.

Dawn is an author and poet. She lives—and performs weddings—on Kaua'i.

Planting Kalo

Beth Marcil

During my career as a visual artist on Maui, one personal experience touched and inspired me enough to create an ongoing body of work.

I was working on sketches for a client commission that would include kalo farmers. I was put in contact with a farmer who was willing to let me take photographs of him and his grandfather working the loʻi, as reference photos for the painting. This was my first real introduction to the kalo culture, an important moment for me.

It was my intention to be as unobtrusive as possible and not disrupt their work any more than necessary. What happened over the course of that day was transformational for me.

Not only was I given the opportunity to witness the reverence with which they performed their task of planting and harvesting, but I was also put at ease by the invitation to stay as long as I wished and ask any questions I might have. The serenity of the setting, the beauty of their relationship with each other and with the ʻāina spoke volumes.

The grandson spoke to me occasionally as they worked, teaching me about kalo and why it was so sacred to the Hawaiian people. After completing my photography, I joined them in the loʻi, learning how to use the ʻōʻō to gently loosen the roots from the rich, silky mud. I walked away from that experience with a feeling of such peace in my heart, grateful to have been invited into the presence of these remarkable men and their deep Spirit of Aloha, knowing I would do my best to convey the essence of this experience and the kalo culture through my work.

Beth is an artist who captures the colors, ambiance, and characters of the island in her paintings. She also works in mixed media, including sculpture-like pieces created from gourds.

Aloha is a Sweety Onion

Leighann Kornberger

Long ago, I lived in a house in the heart of Maui's agricultural community and started a gift basket business with a friend. Our baskets delivered aloha whether we shipped them to the mainland or had them waiting in hotel rooms when visitors arrived.

We worked with local farmers, chefs and businesses on the island to find island-style items (especially Kula Maui Onion products) that were fun—and uniquely Hawaiian. But one day I got an idea. I decided to create a doll for the baskets and SWEETY© ONION was born! I designed his hand to be in a perpetual shaka sign to keep sharing the aloha long after a basket's goodies had been eaten. I even started a website to track Sweety's adventures.

I now live in New York, but I'm still passionate about this little doll that makes people smile. I like to think Sweety is the best part of me with an adventurous heart and lots of aloha spirit.

Leighann is the founder/owner of Sweety Onion LLC. (www.SweetyOnion.com).

Photos of Aloha

Randy Jay Braun

"When you walk into Randy's gallery, you immediately feel at home. I imagine myself moving in upstairs so I can surround myself with art every day and chat with gallery manager Rachel whenever I need a shot of aloha." Barbara Santos

Randy graduated from Occidental College in Los Angeles, with degrees in anthropology and documentary film. Since then, his journey as a professional photographer has taken him from the tension-filled operating rooms of world-renowned heart surgeons to the back stages of Hollywood studios, and back to the beauty of the Pacific Islands. His in-depth "portraiture" of Hawai'i's ancient hula has been internationally recognized with numerous awards and a host of corporate clients.

Aloha and Kōkua

Max Tsai with Ed Tanji

Born in Shanghai, growing up in the East Bay, and traveling through the East and West, I have been to many places where there are verdant green landscapes, fragrant flowers, white sand beaches, stunning sunsets, and serene dawns.

In societies around the world, as well, family is important. But only in a few special places is family the community. Hawai'i is one of those places, where 'ohana is not just the immediate members of the family, but the community.

In Hawai'i, family is 'ohana nui that extends the caring for each other's well being to visitors as well as neighbors; to the newly arrived as well as the long-time friend. It is the culture of aloha that I experienced when I first arrived.

In planning a business that would provide a service for other businesses, the key component is the cultural attitudes of people and I found in Hawai'i an ingrained culture of aloha. That cultural attitude is the essence of the business I envisioned.

TC Kōkua is a technology-based customer contact center. My academic and work experience provided the framework for the business, but it takes people who Practice Aloha to make it succeed. They are easy to find in a community in which the practice of aloha is part of the culture.

Through a decade that has seen difficult times for businesses in Hawai'i and the nation, my business is thriving. I was even recognized by the U.S. Small Business Administration with a 2009 Maui Small Business Person of the Year award.

But no business succeeds solely because of its ownership. I may have had the concept and expertise, but the company relies on the Aloha Spirit and customer service provided by the service representatives who speak for the business. They often are the first personal contact for our customers.

One definition of kōkua is "helpers," with a powerful historical and cultural context in the helpers who cared for the Hansen's disease patients at Kalaupapa.

It has special meaning in Hawai'i for those who Practice Aloha, especially for the malihini who experiences it, adopts it, and feels it.

Max owns and operates Max Fitness LLC, a personal training business, TC Kōkua, and XAM, an athletic fashions business. Ed Tanji is the editor of the Maui News who first recognized the aloha in Max's business plan.

Aloha is a Way of Life

Lt. Governor James "Duke" Aiona

Aloha is a way of life. Through its core values of forgiveness, humility, patience, responsibility, honesty, commitment, and discipline, we learn how to co-exist and treat one another with love and respect.

Let us seize the opportunity that we are provided with each and every day to alo (share) and ha (breathe). In other words, share the breath of life through aloha.

Duke Aiona was born in Pearl City, Hawai'i. He served two terms as Hawai'i's lieutenant governor and makes integrity in government and improving education his top priorities.

The Tsunami Effect

Rick Chatenever

"Aloha" isn't in most newspapers' arsenals of front-page headlines; but it was exactly the right word in the *Maui News* coverage of the tsunami that didn't happen. Days later, phone calls from the mainland were still coming in. People at work and at school were still buzzing. Everyone was still talking about that "crazy day."

There's nothing like a tsunami to get the adrenaline pumping. With sirens going off vaguely in the distance, even Upcountry, way above sea level, we watched the stationary TV shot of Hilo Bay looking for any sign of the wave as zero hour approached.

Then zero hour passed. We shared a big group exhale and got on with our business.

Natural disasters used to be known for bringing out the best in people. In the Islands, they still are. On our little rock in the middle of the sea—like our little planet in the middle of the cosmos—they remind us how vulnerable we are.

The point is brought home especially by slow-moving catastrophes we can see coming for hours, thanks to deep-ocean buoys and other advances in early-warning technology. It's humbling—and might have something to do with how friendly everyone's been ever since.

Venturing out in the hours immediately after the threat passed, I encountered gridlock at rural intersections not used to all that traffic. But instead of road rage, there were shaka signs, smiles, the knowledge shared with complete strangers that we had come through it … together.

I'm still coming upon unnoticed e-mails from Kula neighbors last Saturday inviting their lower-elevation friends to come on up. This awareness that seems so second-nature to Islanders is harder to come by elsewhere.

Like Hollywood, for instance. Still recalling that old advertising line, "It's not nice to fool Mother Nature," I have to admit a small warning buzzer went off in my brain when I heard

Clint Eastwood and company were coming to Lahaina to film a tsunami sequence for their new movie, *Hereafter.*

Oh, sure, the tsunami itself would be added later by the special effects department. The actual filming went off without a hitch for three days in January. The actors—including Maui's eight-year-old Jessica Griffiths—were required to run up Front Street with really scared looks on their faces, then jump!

Jessica jumped into padding just out of camera range…but it will be a savage wave by the time the movie is released.

Speaking now as a professional metaphor maker who sometimes sees things that aren't really there, I noticed that one of *Hereafter*'s producers was Steven Spielberg. The very same Steven Spielberg who was directing the special-effects-laden *Jurassic Park* on Kaua'i in 1992 when Hurricane 'Iniki sent the crew scrambling for safety into the fortified section of their resort.

It's not that I actually believe film companies are provoking the wrath of the gods of nature, so present in the mythology of our Island home. But then again, it never hurts to remember our place in the grand scheme of things. And what is it about us that defines world-ending disasters as entertainment?

Last Saturday, the same TV screens that bring us the Oscars were full of the very real world where we live. We watched flapping fish left stranded on rocks by receding tides, and we held our breaths that nothing worse would happen.

The greatest illusion created by special effects is that we are in control. The most basic truth of living in these Islands is that we're not.

Nature trumps special effects, every time. It doesn't even have to try.

We are like tiny ants on this pebble in a vast sea. We're not the chief, we are part of the flow of life. Those days when everything turns out okay are days to be grateful for.

All it takes is one little tsunami to remind us of this lesson. Especially a tsunami that doesn't happen.

Rick is the Maui Scene editor at *The Maui News*. This story originally appeared in Maui Scene March 4, 2010.

Emanate Aloha

Sally Fox Herrera

Growing up in Northern California as the daughter of a college professor, we had the whole summer each year to travel. At a time when gasoline was cheap and we were being encouraged to "get a Chevrolet, see the USA" my father took that directive to heart.

As each school year ended there would be countless hours of pouring over AAA road maps to plot the best route for our annual foray into the wilds of North America. My father did not have much interest in foreign destinations and firmly believed that the best way to get to anywhere was by tumbling us into the family station wagon at an unholy pre-dawn hour and charging off in our gas guzzler to the first scheduled stop on the highway.

Needless to say, Hawai'i was never considered a possibility for our summer vacations. In my father's view Hawai'i was remote, exotic, and "foreign." Besides, you couldn't drive there. By the time I was a teenager, many of my friends with hipper parents had been to the western-most state in the union and come home with tanned skin, tales of beautiful beaches and friendly "natives." For the first time I heard the word "Aloha."

Going to the beach in California was never super high on my priority list—ice-cold water and instant sunburn. Imagining that Hawai'i had nothing to offer but endless days on the beach (where I would be ridiculed for my light skin) I chose trips to Canada and

Europe when I finally had the opportunity to explore further a field during my summer breaks. Hawai'i remained a distant dot on the world map.

Now, many years later, after a lifetime of travel, career, and raising a family I have finally come to understand why people flock to the Hawaiian Islands year after year. The word "Aloha" has taken on a new personal meaning.

The first time I visited Hawai'i was in 2005, finally enticed to her shores by Will Herrera, the man who is now my husband. As soon as I landed on Maui, I knew that I should have come here a long time ago. The feeling of acceptance, of belonging was immediate. The warm soft air, the clear elegant light, the beautiful beaches where everyone is welcome, warm inviting ocean water and most of all the Spirit of Aloha spoke to me in a deeply satisfying way. Right away, I began to wonder what I could do to give back, to add to the beauty and joy of being here.

In California, I had been running a successful business as a jewelry artist. I created one-of-a-kind necklaces, earrings, and bracelets with beautiful colored gemstones and pearls. I sold my art to support my family and to help raise money for various charities in the San Francisco Bay Area. I was only interested in selling my work directly to the consumer. Gemstones have stories as do each of the titled pieces. Sharing those stories with the buyer is a very important part of the experience for both of us.

It was an approach that worked well and allowed me the luxury of philanthropy. I had been Practicing Aloha and didn't even know it.

Here in Hawai'i, I was finding inspiration in the color and beauty all around me for my works of art and began creating with renewed enthusiasm. The stories and myths of Hawai'i provided yet another creative stimulus. I was making all of this beautiful jewelry and fervently wished for a way to share it with the residents and visitors on the island.

One day my husband took me to the Four Seasons Wailea to introduce me to his friend Kari McKarthy, a wonderful oil painter who exhibits her works there as part of the Artists of Maui program. Kari encouraged me to submit my work to the director of the program. I did so and fittingly, I received a call on Thanksgiving Day inviting me to participate.

Since January 2007, alongside Will, who shows his sculpture, I have had the honor and pleasure of sharing my art with visitors and residents alike. I have found a wonderful way of Practicing Aloha. By sharing the stories of the gemstones and the inspiration for the pieces, I have been able to send little bits of Hawai'i to every corner of the globe—with aloha.

You might see Will and I as we drive around Maui with the license plate that I had made for my car: "MN8 JOY." After all, isn't that what Practicing Aloha is all about? Emanating Joy?

Sally and Will create their artwork in their studio in Mākena, Maui.

Feeling Aloha with All Your Senses

Cynthia Conrad

When I first arrived in Hawai'i in December of 1970, I realized I was in a place unlike any other. There was a young Hawaiian boy sitting on a wall playing the 'ukulele, softly singing to himself. The air was thick and warm with a slight cooling breeze, fragrant with plumeria. There was languorous steel guitar music playing even in the restrooms! I had my first taste of fresh-cut pineapple. The light was saturated with rich colors and there were exotic flowers everywhere.

That first impression has never left me and I begin each day in wonder and awe as I see, hear, taste, touch, and smell all the beauty that surrounds me. It is an artist's paradise. My senses are awakened and I feel such gratitude and inspiration.

That is aloha to me: this sweet, beautiful place and her gentle, musical people.

Cynthia founded her marketing company, Coloriginals, in Makawao in 1987. She is an amazing watercolor artist. Her subjects are usually vintage Hawaiiana memorabilia and aloha shirts.

Aloha is a School Tradition

Rob Shelton

Founded in 1831, Lahainaluna High School is the oldest school west of the Rockies, and it is literally where now common-day education began in Hawai'i. The school is steeped in tradition, history, and culture. Yet, it is also on the cutting edge!

The Makana Aloha Foundation partnered with us to bring biotechnology programs to the school. Students are now able to grow Native Hawaiian plants from the cellular level. These plants will then be nurtured in the greenhouse, and the circle will be completed when these plants are used for important reforestation projects on our island.

The school itself continues to grow. Recently, a part-time resident provided the seed money for a long-overdue and much-needed multipurpose stadium. This person exemplifies true Aloha Spirit and a desire to give back to the community.

The Lahainaluna High School Foundation values the opportunity to serve our community with Loina (Tradition), Hō'ihi (Respect), Ho'oha'ahea (Honor), Kūpa'a (Dedication), Pio ole (Commitment), Kaiāulu (Community), and yes, Aloha.

Rob is a member of the Lahainaluna High School Foundation in Lahaina, Maui.

My Paintings

Sandy Ayeroff

For many years I used the left side of my brain, doing word-processing for several law firms in Los Angeles. As a child, my family vacationed many times in the Hawaiian Islands. I knew as a little girl someday I would return to meet my beloved there … only to find my love was my art!

In 2002, I moved to Kāʻanapali Beach where my aspirations grew into a passion for oil painting. My art is now inspired by Maui, and I capture its beauty in an array of many different colors and subjects. My paintings are the way I Practice Aloha.

This story was submitted via the Practice Aloha website. www.PracticeAloha.org

Flowers and Aloha

Eunice Antosik

The use of flowers is my method of Practicing Aloha. When I present a floral lei to visitors or friends I am saying "Aloha."

I also create the floral arrangements for the Puamana Clubhouse. I am filled with pride that so many visitors and residents of Puamana can enjoy the floral designs each time they come into the clubhouse. This is my way of sharing aloha with one and all.

Eunice shares aloha with flowers not only at Puamana; she was the president of the Maui Garden Club. For her ninteith birthday, her friends Robin and Greg Pokorski donated a tree in her name on the Trail of Trees in California!

Lost and Found Aloha

Diane Epstein

I was making a cash deposit of $1,000 at First Hawaiian Bank. I had counted the money before entering the bank but when I got to the teller I was $100 short. I was very surprised since I had just counted it.

The teller counted it again and so did I. There was only $900, which I deposited.

Later that day the teller called me and said someone had found a $100 bill in front of the bank and brought it to the teller. The bank realized that this must be my missing $100 and deposited it into my account.

The idea that someone brought in cash that they found—and then the bank called me and deposited the money—well, it was a real day of aloha for me!

Diane Epstein has been painting on silk since 1983. She says she tries to capture the rhythm and beauty of the world in her designs.

In the Doctor's Office

Dr. Norman Estin

At our Doctors On Call medical offices, we specifically try to greet each visitor and patient with a mindful "Aloha" and do the same when they are leaving. The word conveys the spirit of a warm, friendly, caring welcome or departure as well as usually bringing a pause and a smile.

Saying "Aloha" also helps us avoid saying obvious or inappropriate or counter-productive things like, "Did you want to see Doctor?" or, "Hope you feel better!"

It helps to remind our entire staff of why we do what we do and live where we live in the first place.

Dr. Norm, as he is known by friends and patients alike, is an internist and urgent care physician. His Doctors On Call offices are in the Hyatt Regency Maui Resort & Spa, the Westin Resort & Spa, and the Ritz-Carlton, Kapalua Resort.

Practice Aloha
In a Spiritual Way

How can you put into words all that the Spirit of Aloha means? It seems there are not enough words (or the words are inadequate) to do the job.

Hawai'i is a sacred place for many people who feel the truth in the tradewinds, see it in a sunset, and hear it in the words of the elders. They practice the skills of aloha to become one with aloha.

Some of these stories are in the voices of people who have experienced aloha on a deeper level than most of us. Some stories show how the people of Hawai'i respect many religions and philosophies while honoring the traditional teachings of the Islands. We find great joy in sharing all of them.

Aloha in Hawaiian Healing

Kahu Kapiʻiohoʻokalani Lyons Naone

From uli (that space in the center of the universe) comes the ha (spiritual breath), which is power and harmony in perfect balance. That ha comes into our presence and is manifested in unconditional love and peace. The purpose of a kahu (huna practitioner) is to promote and inspire spiritual wellness by encouraging all of us to alo (be in the presence) of the ha (spiritual breath). In the Hawaiian healing philosophy, aloha (alo+ha) is the essential ingredient to all wellness (spiritual, physical, and relationships).

Kapiʻiohoʻokalani Lyons Naone is a spiritual leader who uses the title kahu, which means "honored practitioner, a pastor of a church, or a conservator of knowledge." But it also means someone who owns a pet and therefore is entrusted to take care of another living being. Hawaiian culture honors the interdependence of life. It makes little distinction between a human being, an animal, and the earth. All that really matters is that one does their job with a giving heart.

A Prayer of Aloha

Kolleen O'Flaherty Wheeler

My dear husband, Bruce, and I moved to Maui Nei from San Francisco on the Ides of March, 1983. We've considered ourselves "lucky come Hawai'i" from that day on. For most of the time I've called Maui home, I've been honored to perform hundreds of wedding and vow renewal ceremonies (and other blessings) for both my fellow Island residents and visitors who've journeyed here from around the globe to celebrate their relationships.

I wrote the following poem, which I often include in my ceremonies. It's my good pleasure to share it here.

Blessings in the Hawaiian Tradition

May your journey together into the very heart of life be ever blessed with the mana of this beautiful land.

May you always have available to you both the energy and the peace of the mighty ocean.

May you greet one another in every new morning with loving Aloha in your hearts.

May your days contain the sweetness of fragrant tropical blossoms under a hula moon.

When you find life's experiences get a little "hot," may you be cooled by the remembrance of gentle tradewinds.

May every rain shower find you dancing together under a glorious rainbow.

May the sparkling hōkūlani stars inspire your dreams, and may the sun over Mt. Haleakalā ever warm your hearts.

May your hearts be filled to overflowing with gratitude for the love you've shared as the sun gloriously sets.

And, as you walk together, hand in hand, upon the land, may you leave no footprints in the golden sands when at last your journey is through.

Rev. Wheeler and her husband Bruce own All Ways Maui'd Weddings & Photography.

Within Ourselves

Kimokeo Kapahulehua

I am often asked: "What is aloha?" I was not taught aloha. It was what we all have within ourselves. Aloha is spiritual and cultural—a way of life here in Hawai'i.

The more important question is: "How can I Practice Aloha?" Express your love and care for everything of nature and each person.

Aloha nā po'e o honua, Aloha nā po'e o moana, aloha nā po'e o lani. The people of the land, ocean, and heavens—we are one big 'ohana.

Kimokeo, affectionately known as "Bully," is a veteran Kihei Canoe Club steersman, cultural ambassador at The Fairmont Kea Lani Maui, president of 'Ao'ao O Nā Loko I'a O Maui fishpond association, and founder, board member, and kāpena (captain) of the Hawaiian Outrigger Canoe Voyaging Society.

Aloha is a Vital Force

Élan Vital

Aloha is the "breath of life" in its most basic form. Aloha, whether it is called ki, chi, prana, mana, life force, or élan vital, is the spark of life.

The practice of extending this loving vital force in word or deed to another person is the art of Practicing Aloha. Its effect is to endow the other person with a feeling of well-being and being cared for as a valued individual happy to be alive and capable of passing this gift of aloha to others.

Élan is a well-known modern artist in Hawai'i. He took his name from the writings of Henri Bergson.

A Painting and a Story

Andrea Smith

Aloha is the love that exudes each time caring, kindness, and gentleness is offered to another. Our hearts are open to giving because the beauty of these Islands is always giving to us. This creates a lovely uplifted energy that we exist in as long as our heart is open and we show up in love.

The combined energy of all the people of Hawai'i creates a perfect harmony and plays a heavenly song. Gratitude for being able to exist in a place that is a living rainbow of humanity is evident in the attitude. This entire feeling translates into aloha.

Andrea's art incorporates the themes of peace and spirituality. She has a gallery in Sedona, Arizona.

A Purposeful Effort

Theo Morrison

A loha is the spirit that binds humanity together. Aloha is the energy that allows us to go above and beyond to fulfill a shared vision. Aloha is the force that moves the individual beyond self and self gain and toward making a purposeful effort for the common good.

Theo Morrison is the executive director of the Lahaina Restoration Foundation. She is also an artist.

Passing on the Aloha

Harold Kaniho

For thirty-plus years I lived an inactive life away from my religion. During those years a man by the name of Brother Manuel Mathias faithfully visited my home to fellowship me. At the age of forty-three, I decided it was time to return to my faith and did so with full force.

One day I bumped into Brother Mathias and thanked him for never giving up on me. I can still remember feeling overwhelmed with love and appreciation for this brother who always tried his best to help others.

At that moment I knew that I wanted to do the same and give people what Brother Mathias had given me. It would not only brighten their day, but mine as well. It started with a small goal to try and make people smile. It is true: a smile is contagious!

Too often in life we seem to rush through life forgetting to acknowledge those around us. We forget to enjoy and appreciate what we have versus what we don't!

I am currently the crossing guard at King Kamehameha III School and felt honored when I was featured in the article below:

First, I would like to give a positive shout to the crossing guard who is outside of Kamehameha III in Lahaina every day when school lets out. He is out there rain or shine with a huge smile on his face. Children and parents alike love him. It is one of the best parts of my day to see all of the students give him hugs and high-fives on their way out. He is not only great to them but takes the time to give a friendly wave to every car that passes by. That is aloha spirit to me! *Maui Time Weekly,* January 29, 2009

Harold is waiting to give you a smile at his crosswalk in Lahaina!

Questioning Aloha

Rob Westphal

All love can't save you.
Love can't save you?
Oh, why can't love save you?
How can't love save you?
All love can save you.

Through persistent questioning of our self, we come to understand our conditioning.

Once the answers to our questions are the truth, one can bring love and kindness to all encounters.

This is what ALOHA means to me.

Rob Westphal is a seriously creative guy. He is a tattoo artist at Maui Atomic Tattoo in Lahaina, Maui.

Sharing is Caring

Gordon and Katherine Kekahuna

People move here from all over the world to make a new life for themselves. Those newcomers have found here in the Islands that special love that gives them a new life—or rather a meaning to life. It is not the beautiful Pacific Ocean, the spacious blue skies, or the majestic mountains of all the islands.

No! They move here because of the people.

My wife Katherine and I did not move here. We were born on the island of Maui. We grew up with the people that taught us what it means to share aloha: our parents, grandparents, uncles, and aunties. In them you would see their love for one another, see their smiles, hear their laughter, and even feel their hurt and pain.

What is aloha? There is a phrase, "sharing is caring."

It is true. That is what aloha is really all about.

As ministers, we share that aloha with all people: friends, family, and strangers alike. Not only here in Hawai'i but throughout this planet of ours where God wants us to be: sharing our love with people.

It is awesome to live in Hawai'i!

Rev. Katherine Kekahuna is the senior pastor and works with her husband, Gordon, at the Lahaina New Life Church of God.

Learning Aloha

Chris Posadas

I am originally from Oakland, California, but I did live in Lahaina for a year, from July 2007 to July 2008. I can honestly say that it was life altering. It was the best year of my life.

For a time I had not been part of the best crowds on the mainland. I was at a point in my life where I needed to make a choice: take a path headed to jail or make a complete change and head in the opposite direction.

Whenever I had visited Maui (my uncle has lived there for the last twenty years) I was always amazed at the beautiful way people treated one another. When my grandfather died in February of 2007, my uncle had offered his home to me. He saw that I was not living a life that I was supposed to live. After I graduated from junior college, I took him up on his offer and moved to Maui.

My uncle is a devout Christian. I was raised Catholic but by no means devout. My religion was more à la carte. But I attended church with him the first Sunday I was in town—and immediately God had spoken!

This island was where I was meant to be. I began to seriously consider what the island softly whispered through its people. You see, I come from a place where politeness shows fear, and kindness is weakness in many situations. I come from a place where people would rather be angry than smile. Rather ignore than say hello.

People where I'd come from walk with a coldness that walls them off from real human contact. To break down these walls you have to be more than persistent. You have to make this connection worth something, always something more than friendship. There are always strings attached.

Now you may be asking what this has to do with Practicing Aloha. I'm almost there. What I learned while living on Maui was that aloha, the spirit of the Islands, is a way of life that is inclusive of others. It is the giving of love out of love. The simple kindness of saying hello to a passing stranger. The kind act of making food for a neighbor. The words that you offer in a prayer to someone in need of hope.

I learned in my year in Lahaina that Practicing Aloha is practicing God's unconditional love in all of the big things you do and especially in the little things we sometimes overlook. If it wasn't for the Spirit of Aloha I would not have found God and been baptized on Maui. That is the Spirit of Aloha: knowing God and His Love.

This story was submitted via the Practice Aloha website. www.PracticeAloha.org

Embracing the Gifts of God
Rev. Bill Albinger

The values often associated with our Hawaiian aloha—the friendliness, consideration, and kindness—are actually just signs of a deeper grounding. It flows from a culture that sees everything and everyone as a gift from God. Gifts are treasures, not simply as objects, but as symbols of relationship and connectedness.

Aloha is seeing the Creator in all creation.

Aloha allows us to see life in everything. The sea, ke kai, is living and teeming with life that sustains us. It is not a barrier but an ever-flowering ribbon that connects us with everywhere else. The land, the 'āina, is not an object but a partner in our lives. The heavens give us rhythms and a sense of location; they help us find our way.

Aloha is reflective of the unity and balance of Creation. The sea yields its moisture that falls on our mountains. The water flows through the 'āina nourishing all life and flows through the moana back to the sea. The sea connects us with all lands, all peoples, and all life on earth.

Aloha, like the Biblical "shalom," is rooted in the sense of wholeness and well-being that comes form embracing life as a gift from God. This, too, is a gift that flows through us. It grounds us in a place of gratitude and acceptance that embraces others and bids them well.

Out of aloha flow compassion and right relationship.
Aloha! Shalom! Peace!

Rev. Bill Albinger is the priest in charge at Holy Innocents Episcopal Church in Lahaina, Maui. He is also a gay rights activist and supports human rights issues.

Generosity of Spirit: That's Aloha

Kabba Anand

My son Ramoda has cerebral palsy, and is in a wheelchair. We moved to Maui from Kaua'i when he was two because we heard about a traditional Hawaiian healer in Nāpili. His name was Uncle Kalua Kaiahua.

Kalua was born on Moloka'i and was trained in the healing arts by his blind auntie. At the time we first met, he was working days and seeing folks at his home in the evenings. He welcomed everybody, talked story, joked, quoted from the Bible, and used his hands and heart to help people with their pain, their illnesses, and transitions in life. He gave Ramoda extra time when he needed it. He never let us put money in the jar where others placed their gratitude in the form of currency.

Instead we brought him fruit and food from our garden and trees. Kalua overflowed with generosity of spirit.

He practiced compassion and aloha.

Dr. Kabba Anand, D.Ac. has been practicing Chinese medicine, acupuncture, herbal medicine, bodywork, and qigong since 1981. He has served as chairman of the National Certification Commission for Acupuncture and Oriental Medicine (National Exam, USA). He is in private practice in Maui.

The Essence of the Word

Bruce Wheeler

As with a lot of Hawaiian words, the word "aloha" has many meanings, all dependent on the context in which the word is used. Hawai'i's last reigning monarch, Queen Lili'uokalani, summed it up quite well over 110 years ago:

> And wherever [the Native Hawaiian] went he said "Aloha" in meeting or in parting."
>
> "Aloha" was a recognition of life in another. If there was life there was mana, goodness, and wisdom, and if there was goodness and wisdom there was a god-quality. One had to recognize the god of life in another before saying "Aloha," but this was easy. Life was everywhere—in the trees, the ocean, the fish, the birds, the pili grass, the rainbow, the rock. In all the world was life—was god—was aloha.
>
> Because of aloha, one gave without thought of return; because of aloha, one had mana. Aloha had its own mana. It never left the giver but flowed freely and continuously between giver and receiver.
>
> Aloha could not be thoughtlessly or indiscriminately spoken, for it carried its own power. No Hawaiian could greet another with "Aloha" unless he felt it in his own heart. If he felt anger or hate in his heart he had to cleanse himself before he said "Aloha."

The above explains the true essence of the word, in its purest form, and with my understanding of Hawai'i's beloved queen's description, I vow to Practice Aloha, each and every day.

Bruce and his wife own All Ways Maui'd Weddings & Photography.

Gifts from Kahu

Pono Fried

Papa Ka'alakea was a kahu and facilitated the monthly gathering of the beloved elders to share their family traditions and experiences with lā'au lapa'au (medicinal plants). He was one man with plenty of aloha.

We spoke only in Hawaiian to each other (whenever he wasn't speaking to the whole group and when we'd meet in other places). He always had a sparkle in his eye and a smile for you. He made you feel like you were a blessed child of Ke Akua, God.

He was loving toward everyone and demonstrated aloha by being a pure light vessel of kindness and warm understanding. He believed in people and their genuine inherent goodness.

I remember him describing how one should always show aloha to others, even if we don't know the other person. "When you see someone—at the store, in church, at the park, at work, wherever— then you give a smile, a wave, shaka, or raise your eyebrows and lift the head. Say aloha or hello, whatever.... The point is to make contact with one another and be the one to greet them first; give your aloha to them. Then, it's up to that person to aloha you back. Main thing you aloha them.... If they no show aloha back to you, well then, that's their problem."

I was blessed to receive my Hawaiian name, Pono, from him, along with the responsibility to always try and do the right thing. It's natural for Hawaiians who are in touch with their surroundings, ancestors, and spirits of the 'āina. The rest of us have to work harder since we weren't born with the Hawaiian koko (blood).

We can aloha each other and mālama (take care of this precious place, Hawai'i Nei). The harmony, love, understanding, and peace we create will spread out through all we come in contact with—residents and visitors alike.

Aloha can heal the world.

Pono Fried is an educator, tour guide, musician, and farmer.

Sharing Aloha

Piero Resta

Aloha is the welcoming of breath, wishing our friends to partake in the gift of life. Breathing into each other, sharing a precious moment of personal attention where nothing else exists but the sharing.

Piero, a well-known modern artist, founded a living institute of sculpture, intellectual growth, and cultural development known as the Kaupō Art Sanctuary on Maui.

Honoring a Life

Chris Speere

A student in our culinary arts program died suddenly in a freak car accident near the end of his last semester. He was a member of a culinary team that was training to complete their final comprehensive practical cooking exam. The student was very popular and his loss was felt not only by his team, but throughout our program.

The mother of this student knew of her son's love for cooking and the role our program played in his brief life. In an effort to bring remembrance to her son's presence in our program, the mother saved up monies from the collection of recycled plastic and glass bottles to create a special award for her son's classmates.

The mother attended the final practical exam and presented the special awards to her son's classmates, and on that day his "teammates" were judged by a panel of professional chefs as the highest scoring team. It was a heart-tugging aloha moment.

Chris Speere is the Maui Culinary Academy program coordinator. See his recipe for Roasted Maui Gold Pineapple Thai Ceviche in the "Practice Aloha-in the Kitchen" chapter.

Being Aloha

Tracey Ha'ao Lakainapali

When I try to express my mana'o on what aloha means to me, I must admit I sat back from the computer, exhaled deeply and thought, "Wow, that's a big topic." So, as I do when I need to meditate and get my thoughts together, I went to the beach.

I sat there blessing the beautiful day. I thanked ka lā (the sun) for its gorgeous healing, warming rays. I acknowledged the sea-gulls, the beautiful blue sky, the sand, pōhaku (rocks), makani (wind) and kai (sea). A smile came over my face as I realized this was summing up a part of what aloha is for me.

Aloha kākou is acknowledging the mana, the beauty, the connectedness of all life on the planet and in the heavens. Both in the physical and non-physical. Floating in the ocean, I said my usual mahalo and pule (prayer) for its cleansing, healing, re-energizing power.

As a lomilomi practitioner, I am "being aloha." There is no separation between how I am as a practitioner and how I live every day. There simply cannot be a difference.

Things came to mind as I floated and sat there on the beach this magnificent day. I recalled events that personified for me what Being Aloha is—like when people on the beach focused all their energy on you and willed you back to shore safely the day when the ocean turned from safe to dangerous in a second and you were going under for the sixth time. When a friend twisted her ankle on the Kalaupapa trail, walking slowly with her, and being willing to spend the night there with her if necessary. Having the courage to speak your truth lovingly and offer encouragement and options to the person in pilikia (distress) even though you know they then may direct their pilikia at you. Even asking the flower if it's ok for you to take it home; telling a tree how beautiful it is; supporting and encouraging others to be all they can be.

For me the words "aloha," "mālama," and "pono" are all inter-related and can't be separated. To Be Aloha means we also have to be Pono in our actions and thoughts at all times, even when we are alone and no one can see us. We must mālama—care for, preserve, and protect all beings and the ancient knowledge of all that it is to be Hawaiian.

Although I am not Hawaiian-born, my pu'uwai—my spirit and the core of my being—is. My life is dedicated to being the best advocate I can be and to honor and be of service to kanaka maoli, all Hawaiians, the culture, and the sacred teachings. This will continue until the day I walk the rainbow.

This story was submitted via the Practice Aloha website. www.PracticeAloha.org

Aloha is Yoga

Carmen Karady

Practice yoga and you will discover your aloha within.

Carmen Karady is an internationally trained and acclaimed Yoga instructor and the founder of MauiYogaWithCarmen.com.

Aloha is Pure

Mapuana Schneider

What does aloha mean to me? Aloha is simple, pure, and uncomplicated. It is the beauty of living through your heart. It is far more than a gesture or a greeting. It is a way of life.

Mapuana paints with her passion and her love of hula and Hawai'i shows in her work. Her images are featured on wine labels and her largest piece (7 ft. by 12 ft.) hangs in Roy's Restaurant in San Francisco.

What Aloha is to Me

Tess Cartwright

Does one exist if there is no other? I believe most human beings have a deep hunger to know and be known, to love and be loved.

Aloha is to look into the face of another and find oneself.

When we greet another with aloha, we salute our own existence. We are loved as we love.

According to Tess Cartwright, "You start from the heart and go to where you want to be." She earns her living at Whalers Realty on Maui alongside her husband Bob. But her passion is in helping children see the potential in recyclable "stuff" that they transform into amazing art and use as props in the plays that Tess writes and produces!

Divine Presence

Lei'ohu Ryder

A loha is the divine presence of our essence as the breath of spirit, the breath of truth, the breath of our authenticity in the consciousness of love and oneness.

Lei'ohu Ryder is a spiritual leader, visionary, healer, singer/songwriter, and educator on Maui. Her work has been recognized by the Office of Hawaiian Affairs, the Peace Corps, and the United Nations.

Hawai'i's Golden Rule

Steve Franz

Aloha is a spiritual term.
Hawaiians are a spiritual people.
I am a spiritual person.

When I was growing up I had a T-shirt that said, "Do unto others ... then split." This was meant to be a humorous twist on the Golden Rule. Looking back, I would have to say that shirt promoted the opposite of aloha!

To me, aloha is Hawai'i's version of the Golden Rule (Do unto others as you would have them do unto you). The Golden Rule comes from the Bible. In the Bible you find Jesus teaching others the golden rule in two places. In Matthew 7:12 Jesus tells his audience, "Do for others what you would like them to do for you." In Luke 6:31 He puts it this way: "And just as you want people to treat you, treat them in the same way."

Aloha comes in many different shapes and forms and it can be practiced in many different ways. Practicing Aloha is when you put the needs of others before your own. Practicing Aloha is putting yourself in the shoes (or slippers) of others, empathizing with them. Practicing Aloha is treating others the way you would want to be treated.

Steve Franz is the principal of King Kamehameha III School in Lahaina, Maui.

Aloha is Compassion

Ken Ballard

Aloha is compassion, love, light, harmony, peace, and joy, all rolled into one.

Aloha is choosing love in every moment, showing up and being lovingly present no matter what it looks like on the inner or outer.

Aloha is the presence of the numerous humpback whales and their calves, gracing us in the luminous blue waters of Maui.

Aloha is having the privilege of sitting at an ocean-side table with friends, sharing food that is created with love. This is grace and aloha personified.

Aloha is loving someone enough to let them go.

Aloha is being mindful enough to stop and take a moment for another being.

Aloha is an ancient nun in the wilds of the Haa Valley of Bhutan at a cliff-side nunnery, placing two hands together.

Aloha is the ability to say, "How Lucky am I" in so many moments of a grace filled life and then share it with others.

Ken Ballard has lived in Thailand and Bali for thirty-two years. He leads groups and individuals on adventures and journeys throughout Southeast Asia.

Making It Right

Aunty Mahealani Kaiwikuamoʻokekuaokalani–Henry

As a Native Hawaiian spiritual kumu—a teacher of hoʻoponopono ke ala—the practice and expression of aloha is at the heart of my involvements with others. It's all about choosing the energies for either aloha or pilikia (distress), that can and does make a profound difference in one's life.

Fortunately in my experiences, I've found more people doing aloha than not in our Islands. It's a "natural" for Hawaiʻi Islanders —including those practitioners of the ha (the deep sharing and exchanging the breath of life with another Hawaiian). Whether it is through a lomilomi Hawaiian massage treatment or an aloha greeting at the airport with a sparkling smile and a beautiful flower lei, it is all part of the practice of aloha. Love and kindness are special gifts given. The exchange gives us warm and cozy feelings, even from another we may or may not know.

Aloha love attracts more of its likeness. In the wisdom of our kūpuna (elders), especially those who have "changed address" and gone to our spiritual home, their imprints of aloha remain. The word "aloha" is so powerfully kūpuna-engineered in its vibrational energies for promoting love and blessings.

Aunty Mahealani is a teacher-messenger for the spiritual voices of the ancestors. She is also a kahu-priestess and officiates at weddings, blessings, wakes, and memorials. Aunty lives in Puna on the Big Island of Hawaiʻi.

Lomilomi and Aloha

Whitney Stebbins

Even without experiencing the Hawaiian culture, my mother and father ingrained in me the Spirit of Aloha. My six siblings and I were encouraged to be of service to others. Because of that initial education, I believe I have always been searching for the simplicity of aloha, the open spirit of giving, and of community.

During my very first visit to the island of Maui so many years ago, I had such a strong connection to the Hawaiian culture, it was as if I were called to this place. I returned numerous times over the next several years—always finding it harder and harder to leave—only to return to a life of hectic anxiety in the middle of Silicon Valley.

When I finally made the decision to move on from that life and pursue massage therapy, there was no doubt that Maui was the place for me. I began my schooling in the art of lomilomi healing, working with the most inspiring kumu. They taught me first and foremost what it means to respect and pay tribute to our kūpuna, to humble ourselves … to give back.

I am so grateful for their contribution to enriching the life of this once high-stress, hi-tech corporate drone—and for reminding me where I come from and of all the daily things to be grateful for. Those beautiful women embodied the Aloha Spirit. Because of the generous sharing of their talents, now I am able to Practice Aloha through my lomilomi work.

Whitney is also group events manager for Mala Wailea.

Aloha—Something Else

Charlie Hyde

We were having lunch at Māla Restaurant when we first noticed the "Practice Aloha" T-shirts worn by the staff.

I thought of a book I've read many times, *Practice the Presence* by Joel Goldsmith. (He was a spiritual teacher and author who lived on Oʻahu in the ʻ50s and ʻ60s.) The "Practicing Aloha" and "Practicing the Presence" themes came together in my mind.

Practicing the presence of what? What is the Spirit of Aloha? Is this spirit available to man?

Since 1959 when I moved to Hawaiʻi, I knew something different was present, even if I could not pin it down. It was just something else.

In all civilizations, some have recognized this something else as a higher nature. Recognition of things that are beyond understanding has been around since the beginning of time in the folklore of leprechauns in Ireland, elves in Nordic countries, and menehune in Hawaiʻi. There is also a dark side: devils, witches, and other evil spirits. There is good and evil in human consciousness; we have choices.

In my own life, I have made many choices, not all of them good. I have been in a twelve-step program for over thirty years and know only too well you must practice anything—even aloha—to become proficient in it. The end result comes only with many years of practice. What made the difference for me became apparent as I recognized an inner presence that could be detected but not explained. I called this "intuition" at first; then a "higher power" later, as it never failed to bring good results.

Going all the way back to my Bible and remembering people in history who have told of spiritual experiences, such as Siddhartha Gautama the Buddha, I believe that spirit exists and that we can improve our conscious contact with this spiritual dimension. In time, I found that this process—waiting without thoughts, needs, or desires—is called meditation. Just stop, look, and listen.

What became clear to me is that there is something higher than thinking. This higher source cannot be thought, but must be experienced by the one receiving it. I know I cannot tell anyone what this is. I just know it when I experience it. Is this the Aloha Spirit?

In the fifty years since leaving Connecticut, I have not been sorry one second, proving that choice was correct. Unconsciously something was working to guide me, a higher consciousness I did not understand. Watching the kindness, gentleness, generosity, and friendship in Hawai'i has led me to believe we can become aware of this goodness of the spirit within. To me, this Aloha Spirit is the goodness in man.

What are we to practice? I believe by practicing the presence of our inner goodness, no matter what it is called, goodness will express itself through us into the world. We can choose to be kind, generous, loving, and helpful to others. We do not have to consciously know what aloha is; only that it is!

Charlie Hyde came to Hawaii as a stockbroker with Dean Witter Inc. Through a twelve-step program and thirty years of meditation, he now lives happily with wife Elsie in Honolulu.

A Blessing for
Practice Aloha

In Hawaiʻi, a blessing is fundamental to the success of any new endeavor. For instance, a new business would do well to hold a ceremony where a lei, strung across its front entry, is untied before inviting clients inside. A new restaurant or a home is blessed with a chant and sprinkling of Hawaiian salt.

This may be the end of the book for you, but we hope it is just the beginning, too. May you find the ideas and tools you need to live life with aloha on these pages and within yourself.

We pray that Practice Aloha will launch worldwide acceptance of the principles of aloha. With that in mind, we are honored that Brad Liko Rogers wrote this blessing.

In Hawaiian

E kau wale iho mai nā pōmaikaʻi ma luna o neia puke makamae, ʻo Practice Aloha, kai hana ʻia me ke aloha nui o nā kānaka like ʻole, no nā kau a kau. E ola mau ka manaʻo o kēia puke i loko o kākou pākahi me ka manaʻo e laha hoʻi ke aloha ma waena o kākou a pau i ola mau ai ia manaʻo Hawaiʻi nani. E pōmaikaʻi pū nō hoʻi nā lima a pau i komo i loko o ua wahi hana maikaʻi loa nei i ko lākou kaʻanalike ʻana i neia wahi puke kamahaʻo.

English Translation

May this precious book entitled *Practice Aloha,* which was put together with great love from various people, be blessed always. Let the concept of this book be perpetuated in each of us in the idea that aloha be spread to all so that this beautiful Hawaiian value continues to thrive. May all those who have participated in this fantastic project be blessed always in their sharing of this wonderful book.

Practice Aloha
Project Bios

Mark Ellman is a celebrity chef and restaurateur who calls Maui his home. He contributes generously to the island, the state, and the world with both his culinary expertise and his philanthropic work. He and his wife Judy own several restaurants in Hawai'i that attract vacationing celebrities and local folks alike. Mark is one of the original HRC (Hawai'i Regional Cuisine) chefs known for promoting healthy, delicious eating by using locally grown products in beautifully presented meals. He is a frequent guest on national and local television food shows (including the *Today Show*) and appears at cooking events throughout the year. This book is his vision, and his connections and relationships with people have made the Practice Aloha Project possible.

Barbara Santos is the author of two cookbooks—*Maui Tacos Cookbook* (co-authored with Mark Ellman) and *The Maui Onion Cookbook*. Santos, who lived fulltime on Maui from 1988 until 2002, is also a public relations and marketing professional. Her Maui-based marketing company, SANTOS!PR, helped create several signature island events including the Maui Writers Conference (she was the co-director for many years) and The Ulupalakua Thing at Tedeschi Winery (for the promotion of locally grown and manufactured food products). She is currently marketing director of the San Francisco Writers Conference and a director of the Maui Photo Festival & Workshops.

Tehani Kahaialii-Taulava is the project coordinator for Practice Aloha. She was born and raised on the island of Maui and has been immersed in the Aloha Spirit her entire life. She comes from the musical Kahaialii 'Ohana, known for sharing the Spirit of Aloha with everyone they meet, whether performing for an audience or just "talking story." She attended Lahainaluna High School (class of 2002), a school steeped in culture and tradition, where she learned to Practice Aloha through service projects and participation in DECA (Distributive Education Clubs of America) and the Hawaiiana Club. She perpetuates the Aloha Spirit by instilling in others the willingness and desire to give openly without expecting anything in return.

Tony Novak-Clifford clearly sees aloha through his camera lens. He is a commercial photographer who captures Hawai'i's beauty for award-winning advertising campaigns and editorial spreads for clients and publications. His work has appeared throughout Hawai'i, the Pacific Rim, the U.S. mainland, and Asia for the over twenty years. Tony's images have been in featured numerous publications including *Great American Kitchens, Travel & Leisure Magazine, Hemispheres, Island Home, Island Style, Honolulu Magazine, Modern Luxury, Hana Hou!* and *Condé Nast Traveler.*

PRACTICE ALOHA™
Maui, Hawaii

The Practice Aloha Project was created in early 2009, during a time when the U.S. economy was in sad shape and our newly elected President Obama was offering something rarely seen in this country—but instantly recognizable in Hawai'i—conducting oneself with aloha!

Mark Ellman realized this was the reason his decidedly Hawaiian corporate motto—Practice Aloha—was suddenly becoming a message of understanding, hope, and brighter days ahead. His restaurants had always used the motto and it was even on the wait staff shirts, but now visitors wanted to know exactly what Practice Aloha meant. At his Māla Restaurants, the staff started handing out Practice Aloha bumper stickers to customers with a personal explanation of what aloha is all about. Soon the little red and black stickers began showing up on the Internet in photos. There it was stuck proudly on bikes, cars, diesel trucks, foreheads, and one bare midriff!

Mark, working with long-time collaborator Barbara Santos, realized every person has their own interpretation of what it means to Practice Aloha, so he founded the Practice Aloha Project. Originally they simply invited friends and customers to send in stories by mail. Then they created a website where stories could be uploaded from anywhere in the world. The website became a community of folks who wanted to talk about aloha.

Mark and Barbara welcome you to send your story to the Practice Aloha Project at www.PracticeAloha.org. It may be included in the next Practice Aloha book!

Glossary of Hawaiian and Local Words

We have added this guide only to clarify words used as they appear in the Practice Aloha stories. Please note that many Hawaiian words have several meanings. Aku can mean "give" but it is also a kind of tuna!

'ahi—a yellowfin tuna used raw for sashimi and sushi. (It is best when quick-seared in other dishes.) The uncooked fish is a deep red when raw, but turns white when cooked.

'āina—the land, earth. The place one holds dear because it is home (or provides a spiritual grounding) or it is where food is grown.

akua—a god, goddess, or spirit.

Ala Wai—the Ala Wai Canal runs through Honolulu. While scenic and used by canoe paddlers, it sometimes has water quality issues.

aloha—used as greeting (hello or goodbye). Also: love, kindness. Believed to come from the words alo (share) and ha (breath). Pilahi Paki described aloha as "ultimately a spiritual term, which cannot be contained in a finite human definition. The understanding of its true meaning is beyond words." Aloha aku. Aloha mai—Aloha given. Aloha returned. Me ke aloha nui, With lots of love. Aloha 'āina: love of the land.

bento—a compact meal with lots of variety, but mostly Asian and locally inspired favorites. Usually served in a divided bento box that keeps each taste in its place.

chili pepper water—a Hawaiian homemade condiment of water mixed with fiery hot local red chili pepper—and any other ingredients (salt, vinegar, ginger, etc.) to taste! Sort of a Hawaiian Tabasco sauce.

coqui—an extremely tiny tree frog that makes a lot of noise at night. People seem to either love or hate them. It depends on how close they are to their bedrooms.

E komo mai—a friendly welcome.

furikake—Japanese seasoning flakes. Rarely seen on the table (except in local restaurants), back in the kitchen it gives dishes that flavor you just can't quite figure out. Its basic ingredient is dried fish flakes, and it is often sprinkled on rice.

haole—foreigner, white person. Can be used to describe someone who disrespects the traditions of Hawai'i or someone who isn't willing to fit in.

Hawaiian salt—a reddish sea salt (red clay is mixed into the salt). Besides seasoning food, it is ritually scattered to cleanse and bless.

huna—secret.

imu—an oven that is in the ground.

kahu—pastor, administrator.

kai—the ocean. "Ke kai" means "the sea."

kālua—a method of cooking underground in an imu oven. Used to roast/steam a whole pig as the main course at a lū'au. (No alcohol is involved in this cooking process. That would be Kahlua!)

kamaʻāina—someone born in Hawaiʻi. Also used loosely as someone who lives in Hawaiʻi as when a Hawaiʻi driver's license qualifies you for a kamaʻāina rate.

kamaliʻi—children. (See keiki)

kanaka—a man who is Hawaiian.

kanaka maoli—the indigenous or native Hawaiian people, especially Hawaiian who trace their roots back to prehistoric Polynesian settlers of Hawaiʻi.

kanikapila—to play music together. Singing, usually in Hawaiian, accompanied by ʻukulele and/or guitar.

keiki—child. Use "nā keiki" (not keikis) when you mean "children."

kim chee—pickled cabbage that is spicy hot. A Korean specialty that has become a local favorite.

koko—blood.

kōkua—help.

kumu—teacher. A kumu hula teaches hula.

kupuna—ancestor, grandparent. An adopted unrelated elder seen as a grandparent.

lanai—a balcony or patio.

lei—flowers, seeds, leaves, or nuts strung together in a circle. Tip: A lei shouldn't rest on your neck the way a necklace would. It is more comfortable to drape it so that it rests a few inches below the back of your neck. It looks better and the flowers last longer, too.

lomilomi—massage or a practitioner of lomilomi massage.

lūʻau—a feast (usually with local foods, music, and dancing) to celebrate just about anything.

mahalo—thank you.

Mahalo nui loa—thank you very much. Often used to close a letter.

mahi-mahi—a perennial favorite on most menus in Hawaiʻi, it is also called pompano or dolphin fish (No worries, it is not related to dolphins!) It has a mild flavor similar to flounder.

makai—toward the sea. Often used as a direction along with mauka (inland).

māla—garden, plantation, cultivated field

malahini—stranger, newcomer.

mālama pono—take care.

mana—supernatural power.

manaʻo—idea or thought.

Mānoa lettuce—a bibb-type of lettuce.

mochi—a sweet rice cake that is usually a bite-sized mound. A favorite type is filled with bean paste.

mochiko—rice flour.

nīele—inquisitive, curious, nosey.

Nisei—born of parents who emigrated from Japan.

nō—in Hawaiian gives emphasis on the preceding word as in "aloha nō."

No need (or) No worries—both common phrases for "Relax, don't worry about it."

'ohana—family. People lovingly bound by birth and/or marriage. Also a circle of unrelated people who are a person's chosen family.

omiyage—local snacks and goodies brought back as souvenirs. Each island has its own food specialties, so even an inter-island trip can involve substantial omiyage.

'ōpala—trash, garbage.

pāpa'a—scorched, sunburned.

pau—done, finished. "Pau hana" is the end of the work day. Pau hana Friday (or Aloha Friday) is often celebrated with co-workers and friends with food, drink, singing, and talking story.

pīkake—an extremely fragrant and delicate white jasmine flower.

pilikia—distress, trouble, tragedy.

plate lunch—a local style main entrée, two scoops rice, and mac salad heaped on a plate (usually a paper plate). Hearty and no frills.

poi—staple food made by mashing cooked taro root. Sometimes fermented.

pono—goodness, morality, behavior that reflects the Spirit of Aloha.

pua—a flower. Poetically, a child.

puka—a hole (think puka shell) or something that needs filling.

pulelehua—butterfly.

pūpū—a snack or appetizer.

sashimi—raw, thinly sliced fish. Usually, but not always, a variety of tuna.

shaka—a hand gesture used as a friendly greeting to show aloha. If someone gives you a shaka, you can give one back. Here's how:

The three middle fingers are bent down to the palm with the thumb and pinky extended. Your palm faces you; your hand is held near your body. Pivot side-to-side at the wrist for emphasis. (Copying the shaka style of the other person works best.)

shave ice—(not shaved ice!) is a treat made of snowy ice shaved off a block of ice, then piled into a paper cone. It's flavored and brightly colored with fruity syrups.

shoyu—soy sauce.

slack-key guitar—Hawaiian style of playing a guitar when the strings are "slackened" after it has been classically tuned.

Sriracha sauce—not technically Hawaiian, but popular in local restaurants. Warning: This red chili based condiment is blazing hot but totally delicious! Look for the rooster on the label.

tako—octopus.

taro—a plant with a tuberous root grown for poi. Also called kalo.

talk story—taking time to talk with someone not only for the information exchanged, but for the interaction with another person.

tsunami—a tidal wave usually generated by an earthquake.

Tūtū, Aunty or Auntie—aunt related by blood or marriage, but also used for any female deserving a bit of respect and love. (A local child might say Tūtū Mary or Auntie Mary instead of Mrs. Smith when addressing his mother's friend.)

wassup?—What's up?

won ton pi chips—a snack food in Hawai'i. Know those crispy strips on Chinese chicken salad? Think corn chips without the salt and made from fried won ton wrappers.

List of Contributors

Mahalo to everyone who shared their ideas, a story, photo, song or recipe. This book is truly your book.

Neil Abercrombie
James R. Aiona
Nalani Aki
Rev. Bill Albinger
Kabba Anand
Eunice Antosik
Jarred Arakawa
Ateeka
Sandy Ayeroff
Cecilia Bahena
Senator Roz Baker
Ken Ballard
Cindy Beadles
Keola Beamer
Jody Bergmann
Dennis Blevins
Angel Melody Bode
Jimmy Borges
Boys & Girls Club
Randy Jay Braun
Karen Bunzel
Ryan Burden
Isaiah Camara
Dario Campanile
Kaleo Carbajal
Jairo Cardona
Tess Cartwright

Debra Casey
Robert & Roland
  Cazimero
Kona Chang
Ekolu Chang
Kamryn Chang
Lisa Chappel
Rick Chatenever
Ellen Chatillon
Patrick Ching
Sam Choy
Joel Clark Kira
Carolyn Classen
David Cole
Cynthia Conrad
Alice Cooper
Bill Countryman
Chaney Countryman
John Cruz
Nohelani Cypriano
Kyle Datta
Mike deBruin
Frank De Lima
Calista Delano
Dana Takahara Diaz
Richard Donner
Dr. Wayne W. Dyer

Mark Ellman
Senator Kalani English
Elizabeth Engstorm
Diane Epstein
Dr. Norm Estin
Neil Everett
Kimo Falconer
Rhonda Faleafine
Larry Feinberg
"Aunty Kahana" aka
  Debra First
Jack Fisher
Barry Flanagan
Mick Fleetwood
David Foellinger
Steve Franz
Pono Fried
Walt G.
Courtney Galarita
Beverly Gannon
Eric Gilliom
Daryl Gordon
Shep & Renee Gordon
Sharmaine Guitierrez
Manny Gutierrez
Mufi Hannemann
Jodee Haugh

Mahealani Henry
Will & Sally Herrera
Mamo Howell
Helen Hunt
Charlie Hyde
Babymae Jano
Willie Kahaialii
George Jr. Kahumoku
Carole Kai Onouye
Chris Kaiwi
Danny Kaleikini
Archie Kalepa
Harold & Gladys Kaniho
Matthew Kanohokula
Malia Kanohokula
Kimokeo Kapahulehua
Henry Kapono
Carmen Karady
Jim Kartes
Greg Kaufman
Charles Kaʻupu
Dawn Kawahara
Gege Kawelo
Gordon & Katherine
Moe Keale
Kekahuna
Peter Kelly
Kia Kenolio
John Kim
Kimo Kinimaka
Jan Kitaguchi
Ben Klein
D. K. Kodama
Leighann Kornberger
Ried Kapo Ku
Jerry Labb
Tracey Haʻao Lakainapali
Jay Larrin
Linda Lee
Eric Leterc
Dr. Elizabeth Lindsey
Leslie Lyon
Meikaila Makahanaloa

Beth Marcil
Ray Masters
Elizabeth May
Maui Mayor
James McDonald
Trini McKeough
Laurie McLean
Peter Merriman
Mikel Mesh
Maile Meyer
Lola Milani
Tom Moffatt
Stacey Moniz
Erick Montiel
Theo Morrison
Susan Moulton
John Mulholland
Jurg Munch
Lyons Naone
Souta Nardi
Ron Neal
Briley Neyenhuis
Al Nip
Tony Novak-Clifford
Dean Okimoto
Orion
Bla Pahinui
Alakaʻi Paleka
Cindy Paulos
Allen Pokipala
Chris Posadas
Piero Resta
Emil Richards
Leon Richards
Louise Rockett
Cecilio Rodriguez
Brad Liko Rogers
Toni Rojas
Richard Rutherford
Todd & Michele
  Rundgren
Leiʻohu Ryder
Ron Sambrano

Erica Sanchez
Jim Sanders
Barbara Santos
Mapuana Schneider
Piilani Schneider
Gayle Selyem
John Severson
Rob Shelton
Jake Shimabukuro
Lauren Shuler
Georja Skinner
Andrea Smith
Matt Smith
Elisa Southard
Will Southard
Kutmaster Spaz
Chris Speere
Michael Stark
Whitney Stebbins
Ed Tanji
Tehani Kahaialii Taulava
Charmaine Tavares
Maili Thompson
Max Tsai
Shirley Fong-Torres
Rench Tubelliza
Epoki V.
Leaf & Linda Van
  Alstine
Becky Vaughn
Elan Vital
Jimmy Wardle
Lani Medina Weigert
Jim Kimo West
Robert Westphal
Bruce Wheeler
Kolleen Wheeler
Tom White
Alicia Wintermeyer
Alan Wong
Lloyd Yokoyama
Julie Yoneyama
Zariah